FAMILY AND COLOUR IN JAMAICA

By the same author

★

COAL IS OUR LIFE
co-author with N. Dennis and C. Slaughter
1956

JAMAICA, LAND OF WOOD AND WATER
1957

LOVE IN ACTION
1959

PROSTITUTION AND SOCIETY
Vol. I. Primitive, Classical and Oriental
1962

PROSTITUTION IN EUROPE AND THE NEW WORLD
Vol. II of *Prostitution and Society*
1963

MODERN SEXUALITY
Vol. III of *Prostitution and Society*
1968

FERNANDO HENRIQUES

M.A., D.Ph. (Oxon.), Professorial Fellow and Director of the Research Centre for Multi-Racial Studies, University of Sussex, and Director of the joint University of the West Indies and University of Sussex Centre for Multi-Racial Studies, Barbados

FAMILY AND COLOUR IN JAMAICA

With a Preface by

MEYER FORTES

M.A., Ph.D., Professor of Social Anthropology, Cambridge University

MACGIBBON & KEE

FIRST PUBLISHED 1953
THIS SECOND EDITION FIRST PUBLISHED 1968 BY
MACGIBBON AND KEE LTD
3 UPPER JAMES STREET GOLDEN SQUARE LONDON W1

PRINTED IN GREAT BRITAIN BY
WESTERN PRINTING SERVICES LTD
BRISTOL

SBN: 261.62000.2

CONTENTS

ILLUSTRATIONS

PREFACE

FEW parts of the world combine so many features of interest and significance for the social investigator as the islands of the West Indies. The most casual sampling of the memoirs and journals, the political tracts and official reports, the history, poetry and fiction, and, most recent vintage, the reports of anthropologists and sociologists, which have been written in or about these islands, is a fascination. The very names of the islands, even in these days when some have been turned into American air bases and others have become the tropical playgrounds of millionaires and film stars, awake echoes of adventure and romance. And this is specially true of Jamaica, the largest of the islands, with its population of nearly a million and a half, its history of mingled opulence, barbarity and freaks of fortune, and its present prominence as the main breeding ground of West Indian nationalism. Jamaica was discovered by Christopher Columbus and remained a Spanish possession till its capture by a British expedition in 1655. Within fifty years it was turned into a sugar planters' paradise and so, incidentally, became the foundation of more than one British fortune.

So also was the stage set for the convergence, in our day, on an island not quite so big in area as the whole of Yorkshire, and with less than half of Yorkshire's total population, of some of the most urgent problems of the modern world. For Jamaican sugar was grown with the labour of Negro slaves imported from West Africa, and attracted to the island people of most European and, later, several Asiatic nationalities. This is the origin of that mixture of races, colours and classes which creates the major problems of psychological adaptation for Jamaicans of today.

These problems were there almost from the beginning, as one can see from early nineteenth century writings like the spirited journal of that enlightened planter Mr Matthew Gregory Lewis, M.P. Those who have read his *Journal of a Residence among the Negroes in the West Indies* (1815–17) will remember the touching story of the mulatto carpenter Nicholas and his lover the beautiful Psyche. It was about them that Lewis remarked '. . . nor can the separation of castes in India be more rigidly observed than that of complexial shades among the Creoles'.

The 'separation of complexial shades' is a cardinal issue in the Jamaica of today, as in many parts of the world; and it is no use pretending that in Jamaica or anywhere else it is just a silly relic of Victorian snobbery or perversity, doomed to disappear with the spread of education and the influence of Unesco. Deep passions and, more tangibly, hard economic and social interests are involved. Our press tells us daily of outrages and stupidities committed under pressure of melanophobia. This issue, as it appears in Jamaica, is one of the main themes of Dr Henriques's book. He deals here with a subject on which a vast literature has already accumulated, especially in the United States. A social scientist who sets out to investigate any aspect of what is commonly called race and colour prejudice is in an invidious position. He must keep his scientific detachment if he is to say anything that carries weight; but if he wants to keep his self-respect he must not allow detachment to slide into condonation.

Dr Henriques is a Jamaican himself. His study is based on first hand research in a Jamaican community in which family connexions gave him an assigned position. He has experienced the colour-and-class hierarchy from within. To turn his personal experiences into a vantage point from which to examine the hierarchy from outside in an objective spirit has called for both moral and intellectual discipline. I cannot but admire the manner in which he has accomplished this. If he has erred at all it is, commendably, on the side of being too sober and factual in his analysis. However, it helps to drive home his main point, which is that colour and class distinctions in Jamaica – and for that matter elsewhere too – are misunderstood if they are thought of simply as the irrational obsessions of individuals. They are, in fact, social institutions that have developed in quite specific historical contexts, are rooted in stern economic realities, and play a decisive part in the present social structure of Jamaica. This might seem obvious; but it is important to show that it is true by the kind of empirical evidence set out in this book.

There is another theme in Dr Henriques's book which is of even more general interest – a notorious feature of Jamaican social life, found also among the Negro population of other West Indian islands, is what many observers have called the very high incidence of illegitimate births among the economically underprivileged masses. There is a good deal of rather varied information about this problem. Dogmatic opinions abound; and fruitless efforts have been made from the point of view of current Anglo-Saxon ideals of family life, to remedy this state of affairs. But scientific study to find out just what it stands for in the social life of the West Indies has only begun. Dr Henriques's contribution to this task, supported as it is by case material and figures gathered on the spot, is important and novel. It is of more than local significance, too; for the problem, as Dr Henriques shows, is not primarily one of moral delinquency but of family structure. All over the world, today, traditional forms of family organization are undergoing severe strains and in many places the results look much like the patterns described by Dr Henriques. There are signs of this in Africa, for example, both in the new multi-racial towns and mining areas and in tribal areas denuded of young men by labour migration.

Two questions are involved. The first is a question of fact. What exactly is the 'normal' pattern of family organization in Jamaica? This is a question greatly clarified by Dr Henriques's analysis. I will not steal his thunder by trying to summarize his conclusions. What he brings out clearly is that there are several patterns of family organizations, and these are 'normal' in their respective social contexts. For they are associated with degrees of marriage, and correspond to different levels of income and occupation as well as to the colour hierarchy. Illegitimate births – if we must stick to a legal definition which is irrelevant to the people themselves – are an aspect of a particular pattern of family organization and sex mores found in the economically most insecure and depressed classes, which are also the darkest stratum of the colour classification.

Dr Henriques's handling of the facts impinges on the second question. This is a question of theory. Dr Henriques is concerned with the state of Jamaican society as it is at the present time. As a social anthropologist he starts from the principle that the institutions of a society have to be considered in their relationships to one another and with respect to the part each plays in keeping the system going. The system as a whole may not be an efficient or happy one; and Dr Henriques makes it plain that he regards present-day Jamaica as a society in a bad state of unbalance. This is one reason why family organization tends to be unstable and personal frustration rife. But to understand the meaning of these conditions in sociological terms they must be seen in relation to the social structure as a whole.

There is, however, another aspect to this question. The present state of Jamaican society is the result of peculiar historical circumstances, above all of the background of slavery. Dr Henriques gives due weight to the regime of slavery and to the consequences of the liberation of the slaves in producing the colour-class distinctions and the diversity of family patterns. But the slaves came originally from West Africa, to a large extent from the Gold Coast. It is possible that some of the distinctive features of present-day social life in Jamaica are survivals of habits, customs, and institutions brought over from West Africa and passed on from parent to child during the time of slavery.

Much has been written about this problem but the most notable investigations are those that have been made during the past twenty years by Professor M. J. Herskovits and his colleagues, in communities of African origin throughout the New World. These investigations have convincingly shown that many beliefs and practices widely followed in the West Indies are of African origin. Having myself worked in West Africa, I certainly am convinced of this. Dr Henriques gives some examples in this book. What we still do not understand clearly is how and why these 'Africanisms' were preserved under the hard conditions of slavery. Much historical and anthropological research will have to be done to provide an answer. And Dr Henriques's book points in the direction that will yield profitable discoveries. On the theory he follows, if *obeah* has survived for a century or more in Jamaica, with a semblance of its African original, this must be because it has answered to social and psychological needs entailed by the structure of post-slavery society. He gives us some clues as to what these needs may be and I think it cannot be doubted that the personal and social disabilities accompanying the status of slavery had a lot to do with them.

The point of controversy about West Indian 'Africanisms' is this: to what degree are they due to the inertia of, or attachment to the African heritage of the slaves and to what degree can they be explained by the structure of the society that grew up when slavery ended? The issue is clearest in the case of West Indian family patterns. Unstable marriage, aggravated by the economic conditions described by Dr Henriques, results in a large incidence of families that have a close resemblance to a 'Matrilineal' family type. They consist of an old woman and her daughters and granddaughters together with the young – often 'illegitimate' – children of these women. Now the Gold Coast, from which so many of the ancestors of the present citizens of Jamaica originally came, is an area well known to anthropologists for the matrilineal family system that is traditional in that country. It is easy to jump to the conclusion, therefore, that the 'matrilineal' family found in Jamaica is a survival of an African form. But the trend of Dr Henriques's argument is to show that this is not likely. It is more obviously and cogently explained as an adaptation to the conditions of slavery and the aftermath of slavery. And having myself studied family organization in the Gold Coast, in some detail, I must admit that I find his data conclusive on this point. Sociologists will see the importance of this. For here is an instance of a family system, which is still believed by some scholars to be historically antecedent to the 'patriarchal' type, but which has emerged as an adaptation to special social and economic conditions side by side with a father-right type of family.

Prefaces like sermons should be short, and I have already been carried further than I intended by professional zeal for some of the topics dealt with in Dr Henriques's book. As his subject is a whole society in its broad structural outlines he takes in many other matters of great interest and importance. What I would like to emphasize is that Dr Henriques's book has two fairly distinct aspects. From one point of view it can be regarded simply as a descriptive study of a West Indian community in transition. The facts set out here with unvarnished clarity and freedom from jargon should help the general reader to understand many of the puzzling and even disturbing occurrences in Jamaica that now and then get reported in our press. During the war an attempt was at long last made, with the aid of Colonial Development and Welfare Funds, to help the peasants of the British West Indies to raise their standards of physical well-being and social dignity above the miserable level inherited from the time of slavery. Professor Simey's story of this experiment shows that much was achieved but not nearly as much as was hoped. Some of the reasons for this can be found in Dr Henriques's book; and they deserve attention, for a large part of the responsibility for the welfare of the people of the West Indies still rests with Great Britain. It is worth recording, therefore, that Dr Henriques's excellent example in applying the test of first hand observation is now being followed by other social scientists, both from this country and from the West Indies.

But the practical interest and value of Dr Henriques's book is matched by its interest as a contribution to theory in social science. I have already given some indications of this and would only add that the author's modesty on this score does not diminish his achievement.

I owe him a debt of gratitude for showing me what a rich field of social research is to be found in the West Indies – rich not only in the technical sense of the kind of data it provides but also in the moral sense of the satisfaction it offers to the desire to make some addition to human welfare which every social scientist worth his salt carries within him. I am sure that other readers of Dr Henriques's book will reach the same conclusion.

MEYER FORTES

AUTHOR'S FOREWORD
TO THE FIRST EDITION

IN the summer of 1946 I visited Jamaica for the first time since my childhood. The object of my visit was to undertake an anthropological field study of certain aspects of the social structure of the island, namely colour problems and family structure. As a Carnegie Research Fellow I was enabled to spend several months in the field. I should like to express here my appreciation to the Carnegie Trust for the generous assistance they gave me.

An island of over a million people presents a very different problem anthropologically from the small areas in which most of the classical anthropological studies have been made. I tried to solve this problem of scale by concentrating in a particular area in the north-east corner of the island, the parish of Portland.

The data were collected in the usual way through informants, by observation and participation, by questionnaires and interviews. The material collected in Portland I checked against data which I obtained in the course of expeditions to other parts of the island. I cannot pretend that the results presented here represent an exact picture of the social structure of Jamaica, but I feel there are grounds for believing that the microcosm of Portland is a reflection of the macrocosm of Jamaican society.

I should like to express my gratitude to a number of people who have helped the gestation and birth of *Family and Colour*.

First to Miss Margery Perham who originally directed my steps in the direction of anthropology. To Professor A. R. Radcliffe-Brown I owe an immense debt as the teacher who gave me my first insight into the world of social anthropology. Professors Meyer Fortes and Max Gluckman have not only assisted me with their advice and borne with my obstinacy but have proved true friends and colleagues in all times of stress. I owe a great deal to the encouragement and advice of Professor A. N. Shimmin.

I should like to acknowledge my thanks to the editors of the *British Journal of Sociology*, the *American Journal of Sociology*, and *Phylon* for permission to reprint material which has already appeared in these publications.

To my numerous friends in Portland and Jamaica my debt is very great as it is obvious that without their assistance this book would never have been written.

For my wife the usual acknowledgments an author makes seem a very petty tribute in view not only of the help she has given me with the manuscript, but of her patience and fortitude in the face of my moods and vagaries. Nevertheless I can only say thank you.

Leeds 1953 F.H.

FOREWORD
TO THE SECOND EDITION

SINCE *Family and Colour in Jamaica* first appeared in 1953 there have been a number of significant social changes in Jamaica. Independence and the flow of migrants to Britain are outstanding examples. Nevertheless, in producing this new edition, I feel that much of the basic material of the book remains as valid as it ever was. That is to say, the description and analysis of the family structure made twenty years ago represent as accurate a picture of familial institutions in Jamaican society at that time as I was able to form. In my opinion the changes which have occurred have left the basic institutions of the society relatively unchanged.

The complex of colour-class relationship has undergone considerable modification. I have attempted in the final chapter to assess some of these modifications. The original analysis of these relationships in conjunction with this reassessment may provide some indication of the meaningfulness of colour in Jamaican society in the last two decades.

Sussex 1968 F.H.

FAMILY AND COLOUR IN JAMAICA

CHAPTER I

Introductory

FROM Capetown to Cardiff, from Alabama to Aden, wherever the European has entered into permanent social relationships with coloured peoples problems of colour discrimination and social disorganization have appeared. Such multi-racial societies were in general created by colonization from Europe. In order to understand the contemporary social situation in such societies it is essential at the outset to consider two groups of factors. The first is concerned with the beliefs, habits, methods, and ideas of the dominant European group in the particular area; the second with the historical development of the society.

I have attempted in the following pages to discuss one such society – Jamaica in the British West Indies. But before proceeding to an analysis of Jamaican society it is necessary, in order to create a perspective, to see how other multi-racial societies differ from Jamaica.

In the U.S.A. slavery, the Civil War, the period of reconstruction, and economic factors have all contributed, in conjunction with the attitude and temperament of the Anglo-Saxon in relation to colour, to produce a particular type of racial discrimination. The American Negro suffers from legal, social, and economic disabilities. The coloured population of over 12 million is a socially deprived minority subject to the political government of an overwhelming European majority. It is against this background that current patterns of behaviour are to be understood.

The Jamaican situation is very different. Unlike the U.S.A. the transition from a slave-owning society to one based on free labour was achieved without bloodshed. This historical fact has undoubtedly affected contemporary racial attitudes. Another feature of Jamaican society which distinguishes it from the U.S.A. is the fact that the vast majority of the population are black or coloured. The constitution of 1944 ensures that the greater part of political government is in the hands of this majority. Thus the particular problems of the American minority group are entirely absent from the Jamaican scene.

South African race relations differ from those of Jamaica in other ways. In the Union Europeans of Dutch, British, and German descent are a substantial minority controlling both the economy and political government. But the fundamental point of difference between South Africa and both Jamaica and the U.S.A. is the vast majority of black Africans in the society who represent a different way of life from that of the European; whereas the Negro in the New World in most areas has become almost entirely assimilated to European cultural patterns.

An inevitable concomitant of European settlement in Africa has been detribalization. It appears that African tribal structure cannot survive in the face of industrialization. But the policy of *apartheid* in South Africa, which means the social and political subjugation of the African, only produces problems of an incalculable nature. The existence of pass laws is a perpetual reminder and symbol to the African of his inferior status. The situation in South Africa can be regarded as a conflict between two racial groups with different values and beliefs. On the one side is the European seeing himself as the guardian of white civilization against black barbarism. On the other the African, a second class citizen frightened and bewildered in the face of a civilization he does not understand.

Brazil, although formerly a slave owning society on the American pattern, presents somewhat different problems. One of the determining factors in this European-Indian-African social amalgam is the presence of the Portuguese, a Latin people, as opposed to the Anglo-Saxon in North America. The Latin attitude towards colour appears to be far more tolerant than that of the Anglo-Saxon. Thus, although prejudice and discrimination exist in contemporary Brazil, patterns of acute conflict have not developed.

In another African society, that of Kenya, racial tension and feeling has recently become acute. The small size of the European population and its complete dependence on African farm labour, in conjunction with the comparative lack of industrial undertakings, have created a somewhat different pattern to that existing in the Union of South Africa. But there is the same cleavage of manner and custom, of superiority and misunderstandings. The Mau Mau movement of the Kikuyu with its avowed aim of driving the European from Kenya is the crystallization of African resentment at the individual's tutelage and subjugation to the European. In this instance it is backed by a long series of real and imagined wrongs mostly connected with the land. But, as always, the conflict in Kenya has to be seen in its particular historical setting.

It will be seen from what has been said that Jamaican society differs from other contemporary societies faced with colour problems chiefly in the fact that the majority of the Jamaican population are black or coloured with a cultural background which is predominantly European. In Jamaica as distinct from other societies the individual is not subjected to legal and political oppression because of his colour; and although economic and social development have been slow and inadequate they have rarely taken violent forms.

There is one fundamental rule in sociology and that is that an institution or pattern of relationships cannot be abstracted from the social whole of which it is a part and analysed and understood entirely in terms of itself. It must be studied in its relationship to other institutions in the society. I have therefore attempted not only an analysis of colour problems in Jamaica but also of the family, which is the basic institution in all human societies. Such an analysis I hope may make clearer that complex pattern of relationships called Jamaican society.

It is not enough to say that the colour problem began in Jamaica the day the first slave was landed on the island, or that the contemporary illegitimacy rate, the highest in the world (71 per cent), is due to the congenital sexual immorality of the African. If we wish to know the unique how and why we must first go back into Jamaican history.

'Jamaica had the honour of being discovered by Christopher Columbus in his second expedition to the New World. . . .' So writes an eighteenth century historian of the West Indies.(1) From that faraway May morning in 1494 to the present day the European has been a dominant influence in the destiny of the island.

The Caribbean islands when first discovered by Columbus were inhabited by two distinct Indian tribes. The larger islands such as Haiti, Cuba, and Jamaica were the home of the Arawaks, other islands were peopled by Caribs. Today the Arawaks are extinct in the Caribbean island area but still exist as a separate entity on the South American mainland.

For the Jamaican Arawak the Spanish ships were ships of death, for in little more than a century the Indian population had declined from an estimated 60,000 to 74. The Spanish comment is: ' . . . Their bad treatment [*sic*] by the Conquistadores made them all drink

Cassava juice, which is poison, and they all died. . . .'(2) The only knowledge the contemporary Jamaican has of the former lords of Xaymaca, the land of springs, is a few melancholy arrowheads and broken pots culled from caves and burial mounds.

The Spanish believed the New World was a world of gold. It appeared there was some gold in Jamaica which was found mainly in river washings. To exploit this the early colonists used enslavement and coercion with disastrous results. This fantastic reduction of the Arawak population led, as a direct result, to the introduction of the Negro slave.

From the beginning Jamaica had been in a sense the private property of the Columbus family. Diego, the son of the discoverer, had, however, to fight a long lawsuit with the Spanish crown before he was confirmed in his father's rights as Admiral of the Indies and Duke of Veragua. This meant in practice that while the government of the island was nominally in the Duke's hands – he held the right to appoint a governor and certain revenues accrued to him – the King of Spain had very definite rights of taxation and control. The situation became one of endless confusion and wrangling exemplified by official incompetence and maladministration benefiting no one least of all the unfortunate colonist. This curious dichotomy of government between the Columbus family and the Spanish crown persisted throughout the whole period of Spanish rule.

Although the search for gold-mines became, and remained, an attractive illusion it was realized at an early date that, if the colony were to become prosperous, agriculture was an obvious alternative. The island was rich in a variety of tropical foodstuffs and timber. A policy was initiated whereby Jamaica was to grow and export produce to the Spanish colonies elsewhere in the Caribbean and on the mainland. This export trade was in mahogany, *lignum vitae*, hides, indigo, and cocoa. It never, however, reached extensive proportions. Sugar and tobacco were grown but only for domestic consumption. There are references in the records to sugar mills but no mention of sugar as an export. A royal ordinance of 1519 called for the settlement of farmers in Jamaica to implement the policy of exports. However, the response was poor and to offset this a further ordinance of 1526 forbade emigration to the mainland. The fact was that the Spaniards were not eager to settle and farm in Jamaica but preferred to go to the mining colonies, such as Mexico and Haiti, where wealth was more easily found.

Nearly a hundred years later in 1611 the Abbot of Jamaica wrote to the King of Spain: '. . . In the whole island, from the note of the number of confessions that I ordered to be made this year, with particular care; there were 1,510 persons of all classes and conditions, 523 Spaniards including men and women, 173 children, 107 free negroes, 74 Indians, natives of the island, 558 slaves [Negroes], and 75 foreigners. . . .'(3)

This seems to suggest very little active colonization. Negroes as slaves had been imported from early in the sixteenth century – there are frequent references to officials being allowed to import one or two duty free – but it is evident from the Abbot's figures that black slavery had not yet assumed serious proportions.

By the seventeenth century despite their small numbers the Negroes had become a minor menace to the colonist. Time and money were spent on putting down slave rebellions and chasing runaway slaves. Such individuals as managed to escape took to inaccessible fastnesses in the hills. There they claimed to have intermarried with Arawak survivors and to have established their own society. The name given to them was Maroons, said to have been derived from the Spanish Cimaroon after their diet of wild hog. The Maroons became a serious threat not only to the Spaniards but to their English successors particularly in the eighteenth century. They still survive today as a separate group in the society.

Another threat to the welfare of the island was pirates. Sir Anthony Shirley, an English privateer, in 1597 had sacked the capital of Jamaica. From that time on there are many recorded instances of French corsairs swooping on the coasts of the island landing and slaughtering cattle which they cooked and dried for seagoing provender. But piracy at the time of Spanish rule was only slight compared with the importance it was to assume under British rule.

With a small population, official dissension, the constant threat of piracy and slave rebellions Spanish Jamaica appears to have been an impoverished, unsuccessful colony throughout its history. Its apparent lack of importance and wealth may explain Cromwell's action in throwing its English conquerors, Penn and Venables, into gaol.

In 1654 Cromwell began to organize an expedition to restore the rights of Englishmen in the Caribbean. For a considerable period there had been a number of violent actions ranging from massacres to acts of piracy perpetrated by the Spaniards against the British. It was thought that, although not officially at war with Spain, English seizure of a major Spanish territory would be proper retaliation. The expedition under the command of Penn and Venables sailed from Portsmouth in December 1654 with orders to attack and take Haiti. In April 1655 it was beaten back from Haiti. Rather than return home empty handed the commanders decided to set course for Jamaica, 90 miles to the south-west, and to make a further attempt. Jamaica, unlike Haiti, was feebly defended. The expedition of 8,000 men was opposed by a force of four to five hundred colonists hastily assembled to defend their island.(4) Bloodshed was brief, and so on the anniversary of the discovery of Jamaica by Colombus (3rd May) Jamaica passed from Spain. Minor resistance continued for some time but articles of capitulation were signed on 17th May 1655.

The seventeenth century British settlement of Jamaica might be compared to that of the North American colonies. Land was granted by the Crown to many of the soldiers who had taken part in the conquest, and to such people as were willing to settle. Provision was made for colonists to come from New England and the Caribbean islands, such as Nevis, as well as from Britain. Cromwell, now that he possessed Jamaica, was interested in building it into a bastion against Spanish power in the Caribbean.(5) Charles II was to continue that interest.

There were at this time two classes of settlers, the smallholder and the estate owner. The latter in many instances arrived in Jamaica complete with household of servants and slaves. But through settlement in fertile but unhealthy areas great numbers of colonists died prematurely. A feature of these early days was the presence of white indentured servants. These were people who had been condemned to transportation for offences in Britain or who had bound themselves to a master for a sum of money for a term of years. When used as domestic labour they proved their value to their masters but as labourers in the fields they were subject to a very high mortality rate.

Government in the early colony was military in nature. It was not until 1664 in the reign of Charles II that the meeting of the first representative assembly is recorded. Thereafter Jamaica follows the pattern of many of the American colonies in having a royal governor and legislative council, in conjunction with a representative body. It was a method of government which survived into the late nineteenth century. A real or apparent lack of sympathy with the interests of the colonists by the Crown was to be a cause of constant disagreement, particularly in relation to slavery, between the House of Assembly and successive governors – a state of affairs not entirely unknown today in British colonies outside the Caribbean, if for slavery is substituted 'native affairs'.

By 1673 despite the setbacks in the early period of settlement the colony was able to boast of a population of over 17,000.(6). Europeans numbered 7,700, of which 4,054 were men, 2,000 women, and 1,712 children. These figures include the number of indentured servants. Black slaves amounted to nearly 10,000. Such figures are far greater than those under Spanish rule.

Radical changes in the economy of Jamaica had taken place by the end of the century. The original economic policy of the colony had been to attempt to strike a balance between the smallholder and the estate owner, that is a balance between market gardening and export crops – a healthy economy. It was to this end that colonization had been directed. But gradually the smallholder, through individual failure and the creation of large estates for sugar planting, was pushed to one side and the economy became one more and more dominated by the sugar estate. The colonist-settler with his few acres of foodstuffs gave place to the sugar planter with his thousands of acres. As the estates grew so did the demand for labour. The most efficient and cheapest form of labour available was the Negro. The slave trade, in which were concerned both chartered companies and private enterprise, began to assume the proportions of a major British industry The change from Spanish days was quite dramatic. Sugar in the Spanish period was produced solely for domestic consumption. Twenty years after the English conquest in 1675, the figures for sugar production showed that Jamaica possessed seventy sugar works each making between 100,000 and 200,000 lb. of sugar, as well as two sugar refineries. The export price for sugar was 18*s.* to 20*s.* a cwt.(7)

The following account of a Dr Trapham who visited Jamaica in the late seventeenth century gives some idea of the prosperity of the sugar estate. 'The stranger is apt to ask what village it is? – for every completed sugar works is no less, the various and many buildings bespeaking as much at first sight; for besides the large mansion house, with its offices, the works, such as the well contrived mill, the spacious boiling house, the large receptive curing houses, still house, commodious stables for the grinding cattle, lodging for the overseer, the white servants, working shops for the necessary smiths, others for the framing carpenters and coopers; to all of which, when we add the streets of negro houses, no one will question to call such complicated sugar works a small town or village.'(8)

Throughout almost the entire eighteenth century three main strands can be distinguished in Jamaican history. There was the increasing wealth and associated ebullience of the planter which was destined to make him a formidable figure on the political stage in both England and Jamaica. Secondly, side by side with the struggle for markets and increased political power was the series of wars which turned the whole Caribbean into an American Mediterranean in the European game of imperialist expansion. The latter forced Jamaica to make her contribution in terms of man-power and as a strategic base. The third strand was the constant exacerbations of slave rebellions. To these must be added a fourth which began to appear in the latter part of the century – the growth of the movement for the abolition of the slave trade and slavery itself.

But despite the new-found importance of the island in the international scene the planters were more concerned with local politics and the price of sugar in the world market. They favoured war so long as it gave them new markets. The prolonged wars of the century did in fact produce prosperity for Jamaica and other sugar producing areas in the British West Indies. For the defection of French West Indian sugar made them almost the sole source of supply not only for Britain and Europe but for the North American colonies as well.

On the local scene, however, imperial destinies were brought down to the problem of a local militia to serve with British regiments both for overseas service, and to repel French attacks against the island. The government was torn with dissensions. On the one side were the planters in their House of Assembly, on the other the Legislative Council and the governor. The formation and use of a militia meant that Europeans were taken away from their work on the sugar estates which suffered accordingly. The ineptitude of government was shown in the Maroon War of 1728–34, which disclosed gross mismanagement.(9) But the threat of slave rebellions had to be faced constantly – major outbreaks appear to have taken place roughly every ten years.(10) These revolts indicate that the slaves did not accept their fate willingly but seized occasions to make violent protests.

If we examine the economy of Jamaica at this time it seems as if wealth was created as a by-product of inefficiency and luck. The sugar estates were by no means models of efficiency. In the first place the granting of enormous tracts of land to individual planters meant that hundreds of acres were not farmed. By the 1720's this fact, together with the need for land for food crops, drove the government to experiment with schemes of land settlement for poor whites. Later in the 1750's, frightened by a succession of Negro insurrections, the government offered £145 to every planter who would settle a white family on his land to grow foodstuffs. But neither plan was successful.(11) In 1754 the average size of an estate was 1,000 acres, and it was estimated that over a million and a half acres of cultivable land was owned but unused.

As regards cultivation and production of sugar contemporary observers agree that methods were not only antiquated but wasteful in the extreme. Technical advances made in Britain were almost entirely neglected. William Beckford, who was resident in the island from 1773–78, stated that one-seventh of the crop was wasted annually.(12) The planter knew that his market was more or less assured. Why worry to install new machinery or leave land fallow to recover when there was good money to be had for every hogshead produced? With uneconomic methods may be coupled another factor – absenteeism.

Absenteeism took a very similar form to that which existed in Ireland in the eighteenth and nineteenth centuries. The sugar planter came over to Britain with his family and left his estate in the hands of a European overseer or attorney. The social effects were twofold. In the first place the black population seemed to have been worse treated by the overseers. When slaves received tolerable treatment it was mainly on estates where the proprietor was resident and took a personal interest in the Negroes. Secondly as absenteeism persisted and estates began to be articles of commerce rather than plantations to be managed personally, less able men began to come forward in positions of prominence and the general level of the society began to sink. The Assembly was composed of attorneys and agents. Control and government were exercised through the latter while the proprietors themselves were a power in England. L. B. Namier has shown how very real that power was in Britain. The Colonial office in the 1770's took note of the fact that . . . 'From the opulence of the country, great numbers are enabled to live at home [Britain]. . . .'(13)

Let us look a little more closely at this unit of eighteenth century sugar production – the estate.

The eighteenth century buildings on the estate remained much as

Dr Trapham described them in the previous century. It was maintained that for efficient production it was necessary to work at least 900 acres of land disposed of in the following way: a third was planted under cane, a third set aside for the raising of foodstuffs such as yams, corn, and plaintains, and the remainder reserved for furnishing timber for repairs, building, and firewood for the building and distilling houses. In practice much of the timber acreage was not used and became so much idle land. Such an estate would yield on the average about 200 hogsheads of sugar annually. (One hogshead = 16 cwt.)

On an estate of this size about 250 Negro slaves would be necessary. These were bought outright, the price varying according to age and sex; £50 sterling was a normal price for an able-bodied slave. Livestock would consist of about eighty cows and sixty mules. The cows were kept for milk and meat, and the mules for transport.

Recurrent expenditure was made up of such items as clothing for the slaves, a variety of items needed in the maintenance of the estate and unobtainable in the island such as nails and twine; and imported foodstuffs—salted fish, pork, and butter. Other outgoings consisted of the overseer's wages, wages of the European clerks and servants, medical care of the slaves, taxation, and the supply of livestock. Against this was set a gross income from the sales of sugar and rum, which on the type of estate described would amount to about 130 puncheons (1 puncheon = 110 gallons) of rum selling at £10 per puncheon, and about 200 hogsheads of sugar selling at £15 sterling per hogshead, yielding about £4,300 per annum. It was possible to achieve as much as a 12 per cent return on outlay.(14)

The main demand for labour was for the heavy work of planting and cutting in the cane fields, for which able-bodied male and female slave labour was used. For weeding, a secondary gang of older women and children was used. Male slaves who showed any signs of skill were diverted to trades such as coopering. Domestic labour in the planter's house was performed by the more amenable and better behaved slaves of both sexes.

If a slave were extremely skilful at his trade his master might allow him to go into business on his own. In this case the master would supply him with the necessary capital to start, and, in return, he would take a percentage of the slave's earnings. This, however, was a practice mainly confined to the towns in the island.

In 1801 all the sugar estates in Jamaica gave a total production of over 2 million cwt. The population had grown by 1791 to 30,000 whites, 10,000 free people of colour and freed Negroes, and 250,000 slaves, a total of 290,000.

The Negro slave was the pivot of the system and his labour was exacted at times by extreme cruelty. Sir Hans Sloane, the founder of the British Museum, writes of discipline on the estate as follows: For negligence, '... Whipped by the overseer with lancewood switches till they be bloody, and several of the switches broken ... after they are whipped till they are raw, some put on their skins pepper and salt to make them smart; at other times their masters will drop melted wax on their skins, and use several very exquisite tortures....' Absconding merited: '... iron rings of great weight upon their ankles, or pothooks about their necks, which are iron rings with two long rods riveted to them, or a spur in the mouth [a gag]....' Rebellion constituted a capital offence and the usual method of execution was to be burnt alive: '... he was fastened down on the ground with crooked sticks on every limb; they then applied the fire by degrees, from the feet and hands, burning them gradually up the head, whereby their pains are extravagant [*sic*]....' He continues: '... These punishments are sometimes merited by the blacks, who are a very perverse generation of people; and though they appear harsh, yet are scarce equal to some of their crimes. ...' (15)

Such cruelty must be seen in its age. Eighteenth century England was still a place of violent and extreme punishments for a variety of crimes. The planter carried his ideas of justice with him to Jamaica. Perhaps he was more severe on his slaves but then he was not entirely convinced of their status as human beings.

But what type of men and women were these people who were sometimes regarded as trusted servants but were frequently ill-treated and overworked to provide sugar for the world?

The ancestors of the Jamaican Negro were drawn from a great area of Africa stretching from north of the Niger to south of the Congo in the west, and as far east as Madagascar. The majority, however, appears to have come from a fairly well defined area on the West Coast.

Bryan Edwards describes the slave holding factories of the West African coast. The earliest factory appears to have been established at Kormantyn. He states that most of the Negroes purchased on the coast were known in the West Indies as Koromantees. These can be identified with the modern Akan peoples of Ashanti and neighbouring areas in West Africa. The maritime kingdoms appear to have drawn the greater part of their slave supplies from kingdoms in the hinterland rather than from their own people. Domestic as opposed to plantation slavery was apparently endemic in Africa.

Other tribes served to keep up the slave supply in Jamaica. There were the Papaws, who came from the Whidah country between the rivers Volta and Lagos. These were renowned for their gentleness. There is mention of the Nago, Moco, and Ibo. Edwards's description of the Ibo is most interesting: 'They appear to be the lowest and most wretched of the nations of Africa.' They were addicted to suicide on being enslaved, and this, coupled with the fact that they expected their wives to labour for them, which shocked [*sic*] the morality of the eighteenth century planter, made them undesirable as slaves.(16)

The Mandingoes seem to have been fairly well represented in Jamaica. Edwards had a Mandingo servant who could recite from the Koran, and another 'Who could write with great beauty and exactness, the Arabick alphabet, and some passages from the Alcoran.' He calls some of them Foolah (Fulani), and thought that they were, according to their features and hair, the link between the Moors and the Negroes.(17)

W. J. Gardner corroborates Edwards's view that the Mandingoes from Sierra Leone were Moslems. He states that as some of them came over as children they had only learned a few Arabic prayers. Some, however, could read and write, knew the Koran, and were very strict in their observance of Friday. That the Moslem influence was a very real one is seen in the fact that many early Christian converts had a superstitious regard for Friday. This attitude towards Friday lingered on among some sects of Baptists as late as the middle nineteenth century.(18)

Gardner suggests that the term Koromantyn includes the Ashanti and the Fanti. These Negroes had a dreaded reputation in Africa, which the history of the Ashanti kingdom demonstrates. Their reputation spread across the Atlantic so that French and Spanish colonists refused to take them as slaves, though they were greatly welcomed in Jamaica as hard and efficient labourers. But they became the leaders of the majority of the rebellions which disturbed the island.

Messrs Coppels, one of the leading slave dealers in Jamaica in the

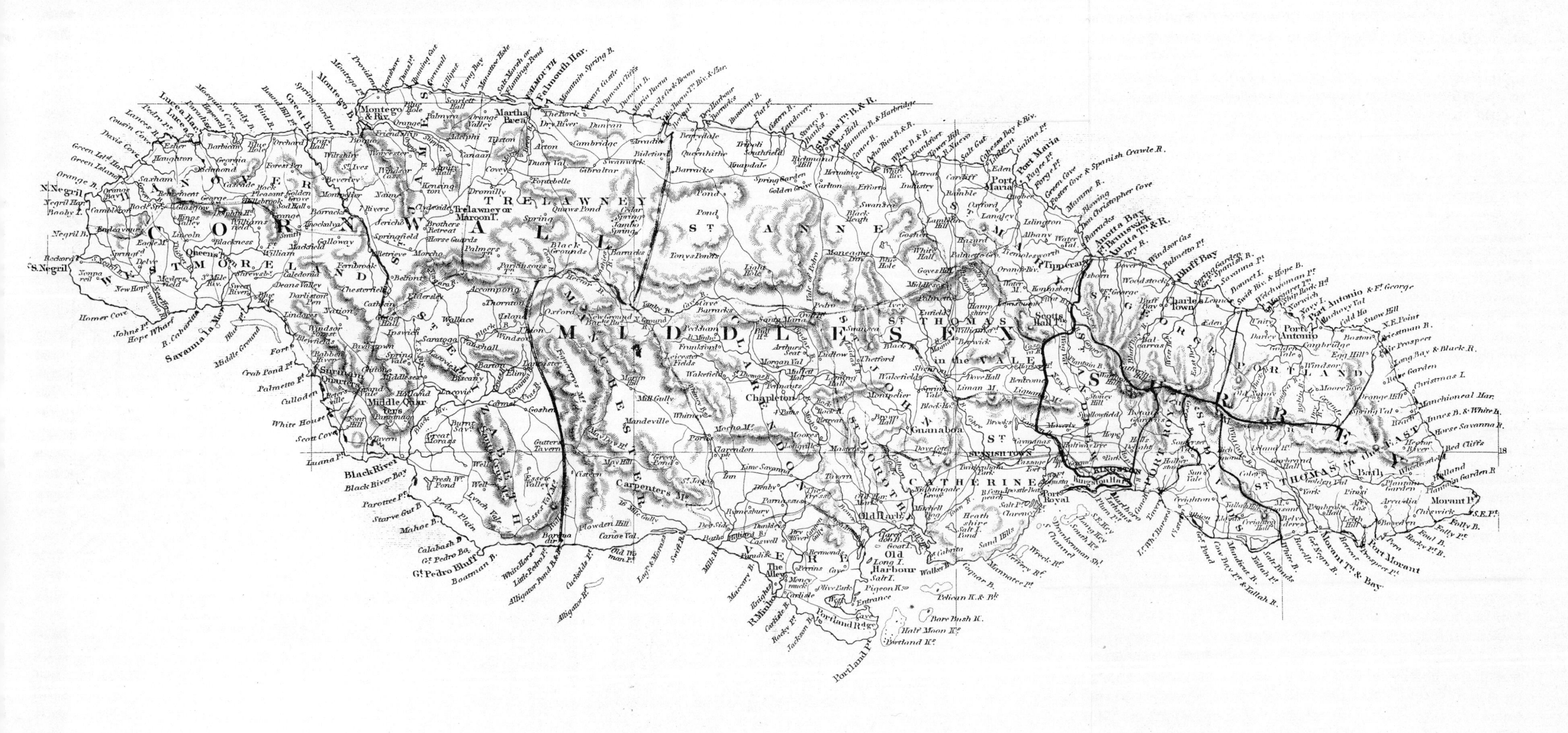

Map of Jamaica: from *The British Colonies* by R. M. Martin, published 1852

eighteenth century, stated in their report for November 1782–January 1788 that 10,380 slaves were sold, and of this number no less than 5,724 were from the Gold Coast – that is Koromantyn.

Mention is also made of the Madagass from Madagascar. They were lighter in colour than the average Negro from the Gold Coast, and their hair was less woolly. In the 1870's in Jamaica the term Madagass was still used of the lighter coloured Negro or mulatto.(19) Broadly speaking if the Ashanti was pre-eminent in the fields, the gentler, more amenable Negro such as the Ibo or Madagass was the chief source of domestic labour.

The influence of the Ashanti can be discerned in several aspects of social life. Jamaican folklore is woven about the adventures of Anansi, the spider, and his son, Tacooma. The stories are very like those found amongst the Ashanti which are quoted by Rattray.(20) The Ashanti word for spider is Ananse, and the equivalent of Tacooma is Ntikuma. The Ashanti custom of raising and lowering the coffin three times before starting for the burial ground is paralleled in Jamaica. Accompong Town in Jamaica, the chief town of the Maroons, is named after a famous Ashanti rebel in Jamaica, but it is also the name for God, Nyankopon, in the West African kingdom. Stone throwing spirits known as Duppies in the island are very similar to the Ashanti Mmotia.

There is sufficient evidence to support the view that although the Akan peoples never constituted a majority of the slave population their influence was considerable on the great majority of the Negroes.

Because of the constant intermixture which has taken place throughout Jamaican history it is difficult at the present time to distinguish tribal types in the population. Gardner says that in his day there were still survivals of certain types but that they were beginning to disappear. H. H. Johnston, writing in 1907, states that he found pure examples of Moshi and Tshi women amongst the Jamaican peasantry.(21)

One of the most fundamental of the cultural inheritances of slavery was the effect it has had on the sexual and marital mores of the island.

The African on arrival was sold in markets of the capital and then transferred to one of the various estates in the island. Later he might be sold to another estate or for transportation to the North American colonies after being broken in to estate labour. In these transactions no regard was paid to the individual's wife or husband. In the slave huts or barracks promiscuous sex relations were the general rule. It is clear that child labour was an important part of the labour force on sugar estates, forming what was known as the 'weeding gang'. Ragatz mentions cases of high value being placed on fecundity due to the planters offering prizes for women with a large number of children. The planter encouraged promiscuity in the mistaken belief that a frequent change of partners encouraged fecundity. Greater emphasis was placed on this aspect of the estate economy in the period after the abolition of the slave trade in 1807 until emancipation in 1834.(22)

For the slave sexual pleasure was one of the few private channels of tension release open to him. Obeah (witchcraft) when practised led to severe penalties if detected. There are still rules extant which prohibited the playing of musical instruments and dancing, which were thought to foment rebellion.

Christianity, which might have led to monogamous marriage, was discouraged amongst the slaves. Although the Consolidated Slave Act of Jamaica laid down in 1793 that owners were to instruct slaves in religion and were to facilitate their baptism it had no effect on this state of affairs. From the planter's point of view owning slaves who were Christians disturbed his conscience, and the introduction of Christian marriage might reduce the mumber of his slaves through diminished breeding. The problem of conscience also occurred among the Dutch in South Africa where it was forbidden to keep a Christian slave.(23)

Another factor affecting the slave's attitude towards marriage was the behaviour of the planter. The planters, as was perhaps inevitable in view of the general social conditions, indulged in sexual relations with the female slaves. Marriage was never considered. The offspring of such unions, the 'outside child' of the contemporary society, were generally more favoured in the eyes of the owner, and they were given household duties as opposed to field labour – they might even attain their freedom. From their descendants sprang the coloured middle and upper classes in the island. This point should be emphasized as it shows that those of the slaves who were in a position to learn more of the European's ways were also bred in a tradition of sexual laxity.

The possibility of African influence on the pattern of sexual promiscuity cannot altogether be ignored. The Akan peoples, from whom many of the slaves were drawn, are matrilineal and polygamous. Polygamous unions in Jamaica are not unknown today. But it is impossible to ascertain the degree of influence which a polygamous tradition may have had on marital relationships both during and after the period of slavery.

The evidence seems to suggest that the direct encouragement of promiscuity by the planters was sufficient to establish a cultural pattern which has pesisted to the present day.

Slavery remains the motif of Jamaican society throughout the eighteenth century but as the century progresses the structure begins to be disturbed.

The era of tremendous opulence when the term West Indian was synonymous with fantastic riches was destined to be short. The return of the French islands to full production, the opening up of new areas such as Brazil, and, above all, the victory of the East India interest in getting the favourable duties on West Indian sugar reduced and eventually abolished, all combined with the intransigeance of the planter to assure the beginning of the decline of British West Indian prosperity by the end of the eighteenth century. In the first twenty-five years of the nineteenth century competition completed that decline. There is a vast literature on this topic. All sorts of causes were adduced and panaceas offered. But the fact remained that the British West Indies had lost the monopolistic position they had once occupied in the world sugar trade.(24)

This economic recession was accompanied in Britain by a new social phenomenon. Men's consciences had begun to be disturbed over the buying and selling of slaves and over slavery itself. In Jamaica the nonconformist missionaries were extremely active in the proselytization of the slaves. Slaves converted to Christianity recovered their dignity as human beings and, encouraged by the missionaries, agitated for their freedom. The planters' reaction was to place every obstacle in the way of the missionaries. However, such men as Wilberforce, the architect of slave emancipation, guided the great movement of nonconformity in Britain and were able in 1807 to achieve the passing by Parliament of the act abolishing the slave trade. This was the first step in the major evolution of Jamaican society.

From this time on agitation continued for the abolition of slavery itself. The struggle was extremely bitter, as contemporary pamphlets showed, for the planters realized that abolition would destroy the basis of their economic structure. However, the days of the 'West

India interest' in the House of Commons were over and the battle ended in their defeat – a defeat brought about in part by men's consciences and in part by changing economic circumstances.

The Emancipation of Slavery Bill was passed by Parliament in 1833 and became effective law in the Empire a year later. That event is as significant for Jamaica as the Norman Conquest is for England, for a new society was to come into being as a result of it.

The Emancipation Bill did not give unqualified freedom to all slaves. It had stipulated that all slave children under six years of age should be freed immediately. For all others there was to be a six year period of apprenticeship which was to accustom the ex-slave to wage labour. In the event the system proved unworkable due both to the attitude of the planter who could not realize that his day of absolute power had vanished, and to the attitude of the ex-slave who could see no reason why he should be compelled to work when he was now a free man.(25) In one sense the Bill defeated its main purpose which was the creation of an efficient society of freemen from amongst the former slaves. To temper the wind for the shorn planters parliament had voted a sum of £20,000,000 sterling to the slave owners of the Empire as compensation for the loss of their slaves, of which nearly £6,000,000 was allocated to Jamaica. But absolutely no provision, monetary or otherwise, was made for the establishment of a peasantry as it was felt that such plans would prevent the Negro working on the plantations. Nevertheless there was a steady drift away from the estates, and in many instances the Negroes settled in remote and inaccessible districts.

The year 1834 marks the transition from a slave economy to a free economy. The planters, however, did not cease to exist overnight. They despaired of obtaining efficient free labour; a fear which was justified by the fact that the free Negro frequently refused to continue to work on the estates. There were faults on both sides. On the one hand to the Negro freedom meant the right not only to choose one's master or none, as the case might be, but the right to establish himself as an independent settler. On the other hand the planter, who had formerly dispensed free medical service (admittedly of a somewhat primitive kind), and had allowed the slaves to keep what foodstuffs they grew, now demanded payment for medical attention and rent for housing and land. The result was endless confusion and wrangling which produced a serious decline in sugar production. The apprenticeship system had been designed to inculcate a desire for steady wage labour on the part of the freed Negro. Unfortunately due to the intransigeance of the planter it proved a failure and was abandoned. The planters later adopted the device of importing indentured labour from India as a labour force. This scheme proved to be a success in both Trinidad and British Guiana but was only moderately successful in Jamaica.

But the year 1834 did not only produce negative results in the passing of an economy. A new phenomenon occurred in the emergence of a peasantry. As stated above the compensation given to the planters had been entirely for their own use. No effort was made by the government to encourage the growth of peasant proprietors. That they did emerge as a new class in the society was largely due to the efforts of the nonconformist missionary organizations which had been in the forefront of the fight against slavery, and to the efforts of the Negroes themselves.

The planters did everything they could to discourage the growth of the peasant class, as they saw in it a serious threat to the economic structure of the estate. They refused to sell land to individuals in small lots. This was met by the purchase of large sections of land by missionary bodies, which then sold or leased it in small lots to individual Negroes. In this way, and also by the activity of squatters taking land in inaccessible places in the hills, a substantial peasant group came into being.(26)

But not all Negroes were able to become peasant proprietors. Many for one reason or another were unable to leave the estates, and they remained as wage labourers engaged in a perpetual fight to pay their rent and feed their families. Some tended to drift from estate to estate in search of better conditions. They became that landless proletariat which is such a familiar phenomenon in the contemporary scene.

A distinguishing mark of the post-emancipation economy was the development of a free internal market.(27) This was and still is in the hands of the Jamaican peasant folk. Freedom meant that the individual could now travel from one end of the island to the other. A sturdy marketing network system developed all over the island and was quickly dominated by women. The modern 'higgler' or market seller in Jamaica today is nearly always a woman.

The latter part of the nineteenth century presented the picture of an unbalanced economy. The planter was still striving to maintain his position as the supplier of a single commodity in an international market beset by other producers in different areas. The new peasant class was endeavouring to build up what was in fact an internal peasant economy. And at the same time there was the landless rural proletariat – the wage-slave – at the mercy of the planters.

Jamaica had throughout this period continued with its eighteenth century forms of government; governor, nominated Legislative Council, and elected House of Assembly. Obviously the Assembly had only agreed to emancipation under duress from the Imperial Government. Its representatives were still elected on a narrow European franchise, and still remained in control of local affairs. The vicissitudes of the post-emancipation period were increased by the inefficiency of this body and its indifference to problems vital to the social and economic welfare of the society. Enlightened governors, as during the previous century, were perpetually faced with the self-centred opposition of the planters. This state of affairs culminated in the so-called Jamaica Rebellion of 1865. Protest and agitation at misgovernment and neglect led to a fragmentary outbreak in a single parish. The governor at the time, Edward Eyre, became unduly alarmed and retaliated with savage reprisals.(28) Eventually he was recalled and the following year the Assembly voted itself out of existence, a somewhat unique event in the history of colonial legislatures. Abuses in local government were corrected and the constitution was modified to permit of much greater control by the Colonial Office.

A shift in the economic unbalance of the nineteenth century came when banana cultivation was introduced by American enterprise in 1867. Progress began towards a sounder economy. The banana is a crop which does not require intensive cultivation and so it is eminently suitable as a peasant crop. But it is also a peasant crop which can be exported.

The banana was not only taken up by the peasants but also by the landlords and many sugar estates were turned over to this crop. Individual proprietors began to give way to blocs of company financed estates which are a feature of the contemporary economic structure. These company estates are now mainly owned by American and British interests.

Despite this change there has been a continued growth of a landless proletariat. The government has been forced to adopt various schemes of land settlement in an endeavour to provide these people with holdings which will at least give them a means of subsistence. The method is for the government to buy a large estate and divide it up into lots of varying sizes. Individuals are able to rent or lease lots on favourable terms. Loans can be obtained from agricultural banks for this purpose. To see that the land is properly farmed there is a government supervisor in residence. During the late war the government went into business as a bulk buyer of foodstuffs, and the peasant was thus assured of a guaranteed market for his products.

The contemporary economy is based on the export of rum, sugar, and bananas. Sugar still remains a large estate crop, and is produced on either the individually or company owned estate. Banana production is divided between the large estates and the peasant proprietor. The internal market for produce is very active. Today there is still a comparatively large unemployment problem despite the schemes of land settlement. It has been estimated that out of a population of 1,237,063 there are 30,000 adults and their dependants without means of support. Government revenue is largely derived from a variety of import duties.

This picture is essentially unbalanced.

On the one side there is the individual who is engaged in business and who may in addition own an estate or several estates. In conjunction with him is the company similarly engaged. These two constitute a very small minority. Opposed to them is the landless peasant or townsman who lives in the most abject poverty and gains his livelihood as best he may, possibly as a migrant worker from one sugar estate to another in the crop season. Between these two is the peasant proprietor who may struggle just above the poverty line with his holding of less than an acre, or who may possess more than a hundred acres and thus the means of a reasonable living. Associated with the comparatively rich peasant is the small business proprietor or individual professional man.

It is a structure which, by reason of its great extremes of wealth and poverty, is intrinsically unhealthy.

Politically the twentieth century has contributed the second outstanding event in the history of Jamaica. As a result of riots and disturbances throughout the British West Indian area in the late thirties a Royal Commission was sent out in 1938 to investigate conditions. Its report gives an extraordinarily vivid picture of the poverty and distress in the British Caribbean.(29) Two major reforms stemmed from this report. The first was the granting to Jamaica of a new constitution (1944) based on universal adult suffrage, which ensured a much greater control of their affairs to the people of

Jamaica than ever before. The second applied to the whole Colonial Empire. This was the setting up of Colonial Development and Welfare as an agency to assist colonial governments in preparing projects to improve their economies and to help finance such schemes. This agency is financed by funds granted by the Imperial Government. As the Colonial Secretary of the day, Oliver Stanley, said in reference to the West Indies, this was some recompense for the neglect of the people at the time of emancipation.

It is a far cry from the landfall of Columbus in 1494 to the constitution of 1944. I have attempted very briefly to trace the outline of the social and historical development of Jamaican society. For, as I said above, to understand the contemporary patterns of behaviour it is first necessary to have looked at the origins and bases of the present-day social phenomena. That, however inadequately, I have tried to do.

NOTES AND REFERENCES

1. Bryan Edwards, *History of the West Indies*, Third Edition, London, 1801, Vol. I, p. 152.
2. F. Cundall and J. L. Pietersz, *Jamaica Under the Spaniards*, Jamaica, 1919, p. 49
3. Ibid., p. 34.
4. Ibid., p. 51, and W. J. Gardner, *History of Jamaica*, London, 1909, p. 30.
5. T. Carlyle, *Letters of Oliver Cromwell*, London, 1870, Vol. IV, Letters cciv–ccvi.
6. Gardner, op. cit., p. 60.
7. Ibid., p. 85
8. Quoted by Gardner, op. cit., p. 86.
9. H. Dallas, *History of the Maroon War*, London, 1790, p. 53.
10. Gardner, op. cit., pp. 132–6, and L. J. Ragatz, *The Fall of the Planter Class in the British Caribbean*, N.Y., 1963, p. 31.
11. Gardner, op. cit., p. 160.
12. William Beckford, *A Descriptive Account of the Island of Jamaica*, 1790, p. 59.
13. L. B. Namier, *England in the Age of the American Revolution*, London, 1930, pp. 271–80.
14. Bryan Edwards, *History . . . of the British Colonies in the West Indies*,

Third Edition, London, 1801, Vol. II, p. 297; and L. J. Ragatz, op. cit., p. 307.
15. Sir Hans Sloane, *A Voyage to the Islands . . . and Jamaica*, London, 1707–25, p. 153.
16. Edwards, op. cit., pp. 62–9, 70, 88–9.
17. Ibid., pp. 72–3.
18. Gardner, op. cit., p. 175.
19. Ibid., p. 97
20. R. S. Rattray, *Akan-Ashanti Folk-Tales*, Oxford, 1930.
21. H. H. Johnston, *The Negro in the New World*, London, 1910, pp. 275–6.
22. Ragatz, op. cit., pp. 35–6.
23. I. D. MacCrone, *Race Attitudes in South Africa*, Oxford, 1937, p. 41.
24. The best accounts of the sugar economy are contained in L. J. Ragatz, op. cit., pp. 37–80, and Eric Williams, *Slavery and Capitalism*, Chapel Hill, 1944.
25. W. L. Burn, *Emancipation and Apprenticeship in the British West Indies*, London, 1937, p. 366.
26. H. Paget, 'Free Village System in Jamaica', *Jamaican Historical Review*, Vol. I, No. 1.
27. Lord Olivier, *Jamaica : The Blessed Island*, London, 1936, p. 159.
28. The best analysis of the Jamaica Rebellion is that given by Lord Olivier in *The Myth of Governor Eyre*, London, 1933. For a view opposed to Olivier's see G. Dutton, *The Hero as Murderer*, London, 1967.
29. *Report of the Royal West India Commission*, H.M.S.O., London, 1945.

CHAPTER II

The Origins of the Colour-class System

UNDER the system of slavery there was a definite process of selection with regard to the employment of the slave. The more gentle and amenable of the Negroes were employed as personal or domestic servants. Another pattern of great frequency was the choice by the planter of the more comely of the female slaves as his concubines. It was in these two categories: domestic slaves, and concubines and their progeny, that manumission in the period of slavery was mostly practised.

Manumission was the legal device for setting a slave free. It was natural that the planter should desire to free his concubine and the children she had borne him. But that miscegenation had become a social problem in the eighteenth century is borne out by an inquiry of the Jamaica Assembly in 1763 into the amount of property which had been left to coloured children. Such property was estimated to be valued at £2–3,000,000. The fear of the growth of a strong, wealthy coloured population led to the passing of an act declaring that a devise from a white to a Negro or mulatto (coloured person) should not exceed £1,200.(1)

But there were other means of checking the rise of the coloured class.

It had been enacted almost from the founding of the colony that the Negro slave and the freedman were to be regarded as the legal inferior of the white man. As a freedman the black or mulatto was denied all social rights enjoyed by the whites. For example his evidence in a court of law was not acceptable against that of a white.

But there were certain exceptions which served to create a division between the black and the coloured freedman. The Assembly passed acts from time to time admitting that a particular individual of colour was a freedman with special rights. These people, whose number was very small, were manumitted by private acts of the Assembly, and were allowed all the privileges of the whites, except that of membership of the Assembly, and of serving as justices or jurymen. They were generally confined to those who had inherited property from their white fathers.(2)

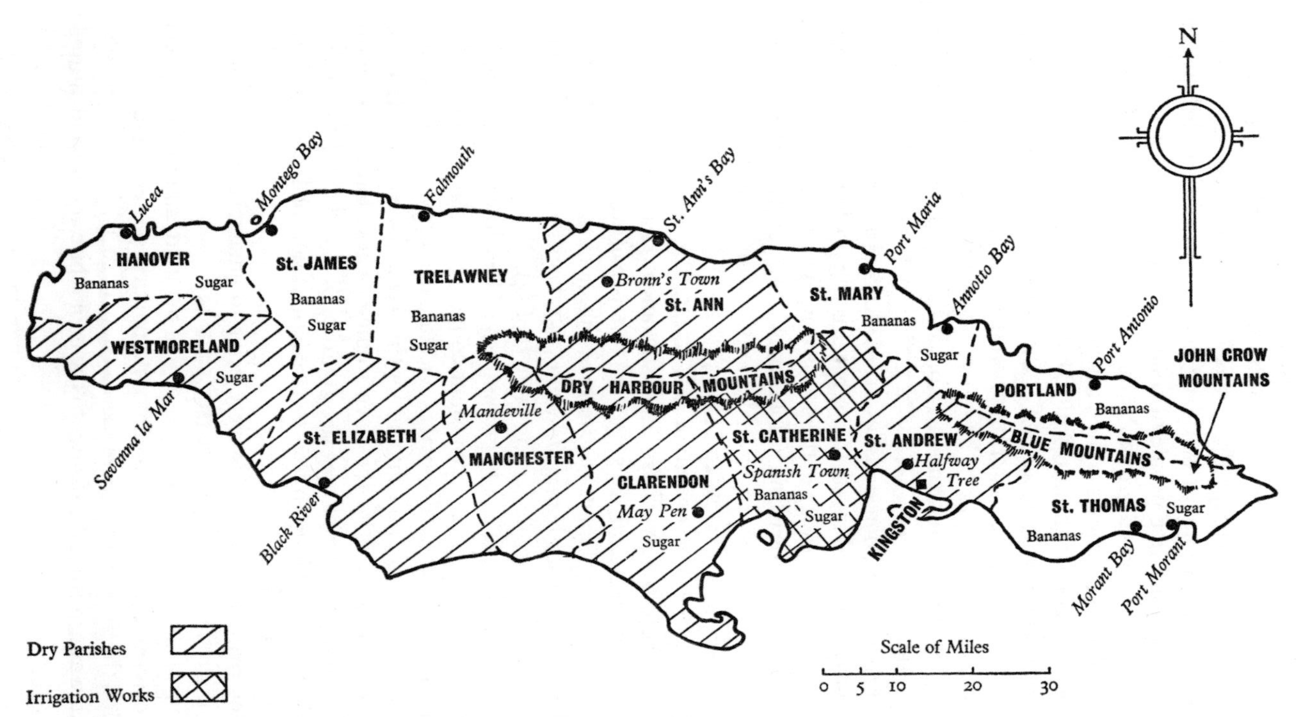

Map of Jamaica showing chief towns, parishes and areas of banana and sugar production

An act of 1748 had, however, permitted Negroes who had been freedmen for more than six months to give evidence against free people of colour, except those specially exempt. But the fact remained that legal support was given to the distinction made between free Negroes and free people of colour.

Inside the coloured group distinctions had grown up very early. Sir Hans Sloane, writing in the early years of the eighteenth century, divides the population into: white; blacks; mulattoes – the offspring of white and black; quadroons – the offspring of mulattoes and whites; mustees – the offspring of whites and quadroons. The last category felt themselves to be nearest to the whites in appearance, behaviour, and thought, and therefore at the top of the coloured hierarchy. And indeed they were so regarded by the other categories.

In pre-emancipation statistics, freed Negroes and people of colour were often classified together, so that it is impossible to arrive at the proportion of each group in the population. An estimate of 1791 gives the population of the island as follows: whites, 30,000; freed Negroes and people of colour, 10,000; Maroons, about 1,400; Negro slaves, 250,000, giving a total of 291,400.(3)

Reasons for miscegenation are clear. In eighteenth-century Jamaica there were very few Englishwomen. Henry Long, another historian of the island, says that the number of women was far less than the number of men. He speaks of the shock to the newly arrived in the colony to see legitimate white and illegitimate coloured children living together under the same roof.(4)

There was also the fact of propinquity. The white man, during his work on the estate, was in constant contact with slave women, who were completely at his disposal as rejection of an advance of this kind might lead to severe punishment for the slave. Concubinage brought very real advantages to the slave women. These took the form of relief from field labour and the granting of a variety of privileges. Ultimately it might even lead to freedom, if not for herself, at least for her children.

The planter-dominated society prior to emancipation was of an essentially hierarchical nature (see page 45).

The planters stood at the apex of this pyramid, and in their hands was concentrated all the economic and political power in the society. Within the white group there was a system of social gradings stretching downward from the planter to the poor white and the indentured servant.

The whites who directed affairs in the Assembly were made up of planters, attorneys, and men of business. These formed the highest category, and they were virtually in control of the destiny of the island. Below them came a group composed of book-keepers or managers, and in the lowest category were the poor whites who farmed a few acres. But however low the white might be in the white scale he was nevertheless the superior of any man of colour, or Negro. His position was reinforced by law and custom as a completely free individual with certain rights, duties, and obligations denied to all non-whites.

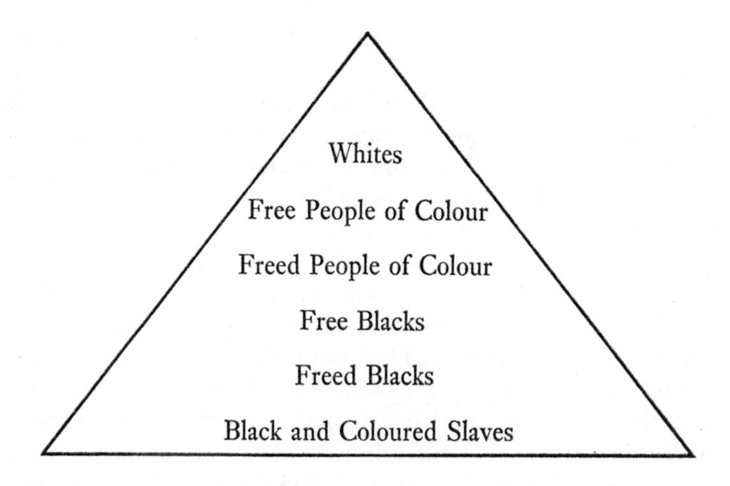

The poor whites had been, or were descendants of, indentured or bond servants, that is convicts who were assigned to planters to work in conditions very akin to slavery for a period of years. At the end of their sentence very many of them established cultivations which grew foodstuffs for local consumption. Their descendants have remained a depressed class to this day.(5) The unity within this group was and is provided by colour.

As the hierarchical ladder is descended the next group is that of the free coloured – those born free; the freed coloured – those manumitted; the free blacks; the freed blacks. Unlike the whites the social gradings within each of these groups were not only determined by occupation or income but by actual skin colour and features. Those nearest to the whites in appearance were accounted superior to those whose appearance was more negroid, and so down to the full blooded Negro.

Many individuals in these categories of ex-slaves who had now become slave owners appear to have been noted for an even greater cruelty towards their slaves than characterized the white planters. To understand such behaviour it is necessary to realize that both the freed and free blacks, and the coloured people sought to offset their colour and all that it connoted by an excessive imitation of the white's behaviour, manner, and dress. Solicitude for the slaves might have been construed as an act of identification with the lowest group in the society.

The base of the pyramid was provided by the largest group in the population, that of the black and coloured slaves. Even within this group there was indication of some social grading. Those individuals whose colour or occupation was held to be inferior, as in the case of the black field slave, ranked below those who were distinguished by domestic work and lightness of complexion.

The society can thus be seen as a series of three groups, each divided within itself, whether by colour or occupation, into a hierarchical system. All the real power lay within the white group which was supported by law and armed force. The whole economic strength of the society depended on the black slave. But these groups were not independent of each other – they were mutually interdependent. Yet despite the web of social relationships which joined them, physical intimacy, affection, even tenderness could not diminish the social distance that lay between master and slave, between the white man and his concubine and coloured progeny.

M. G. Lewis, in his *Journal of a West India Proprietor*, published in the 1820's, has this entry for January 15th: 'The offspring of a white man and a black woman is a mulatto; the mulatto and black produce a sambo; from a mulatto and white comes the quadroon; from the quadroon and white comes the mustee; the child of a mustee by a white man is called a musteffino, while the children of a musteffino are free by law, and rank as white persons to all intents and purposes. . . .' Mulatto and sambo are the only two of these terms in current use in Jamaica.

The balls which were held by the coloured groups illustrate one effect that social segregation had on these people. According to Lewis and W. J. Gardner, these were elaborate dances to which only coloured people were admitted. Others were held to which only fair coloured girls and white men came. These last seem to have been similar to the famous octoroon balls of New Orleans, and to have served the same function – that of permitting white men to choose their future mistresses.

The history of the times shows that at no period did white men experience difficulty in obtaining concubines from amongst coloured women. This was due to the fact that irrespective of their economic position coloured women felt that marriage with a coloured man could never give them the prestige and protection that an illegal union with a white man conferred.

In the early years of the nineteenth century the position of free Negroes and people of colour showed a definite improvement. In 1816 the Assembly decreed that manumission by will was to be legal. Prior to this it had had to take place in the lifetime of the owner. In 1824 free Negroes and people of colour were allowed to give evidence in a court of law against whites. Both these concessions were given after the abolition of the slave trade and at a time when opinion in Britain was running very much in favour of the Negroes.

After emancipation the same lines of distinction were carried over into the new free society. The black man still remained at the bottom of the social ladder, and the coloured groups still maintained their general superiority to the black, and were themselves treated as inferior by the whites.

By this time the coloured group was beginning to vie with the white planters for economic power, but although individuals might often be the equal or even the superior of the whites in terms of property, they were never accepted as social equals. The black section was economically the weakest in the community. The freedom of the Negro meant no change for him in the hierarchical system.

The whole system was reinforced and maintained by the traditions of slavery which had placed the European in the position of supreme power and authority, and the black man in the position of a chattel. Emancipation may have given freedom to the black and coloured people, but the white men still managed to retain a great deal of economic and political control.

In 1865, the year of the Jamaica Rebellion, only 1,903 out of a population of 440,000 had a vote. Of that number only a tiny fraction was coloured or black.(6)

After the rebellion the black and coloured peoples, as they grew in economic strength, began to play a greater part in public affairs.

In 1907 the Legislative Council was composed of four Europeans, four Jamaica-Jewish, one full-blooded Negro, and five coloured men.(7)

Although there were great advances in the spheres of politics and economics the black and coloured groups remained, as they remain today, the social inferiors of the white group. Only one change is noticeable, which is in regard to the poor whites. After emancipation their economic position was very little different from that of the Negro, and gradually they have become recognized by the society as the social equals of the Negro.

The fact that the coloured group had been favoured from a remote period, that it had been able to profit by education and monetary advantages denied to the black man, and above all, that in appearance it was nearer to the white minority, was sufficient for it to consolidate its position as a social group midway between the white and the black.

A social change of great importance after the abolition of slavery was the gradual lessening of the incidence of concubinage, and the beginning of marriages between the whites and the very fair coloured section of the population. This has had a considerable effect on white-coloured attitudes.

During the whole post-emancipation period the coloured people have been encouraged and favoured by successive governments on the one hand, while on the other the quasi-endogamous white group has denied them complete social equality.

After the emancipation the government adopted the expedient of importing indentured labour from India in order to offset the dwindling supply of labour. The fact that the East Indians were prepared to work on the sugar estates in conditions little removed from slavery led the blacks to view them with the greatest contempt. This feeling still exists today. The majority of Indians, after serving their indentures, remain as peasant cultivators just above the poverty line. In the Jamaican population of 1,273,063 East Indians number 26,507.

The scheme of importing labour from India was first adopted in 1845 and lasted only a few years. It was tried again for a brief time in 1860 and 1869, but it was never really a success. In Trinidad, however, the Indians proved excellent workers and immigration did not cease till 1917.

Some Chinese arrived in Jamaica from Panama in 1854 as indentured labour. Later more were brought from Hong Kong in 1884.

Unlike the Indians they have completely left the pursuit of agriculture, and today they largely dominate the retail grocery trade. In every village in Jamaica there is a shop run by a Chinese. There are 12,394 Chinese in the island today.

Syrians came over as visitors to the Jamaica Exhibition in 1891, and remained to promote business enterprises mostly connected with the clothing trade. Later others came as pedlars, and many gradually built up flourishing businesses.

There has been a small Portuguese and German-Jewish settlement in Jamaica since the early sixteenth century when Diego, Columbus's son, offered them asylum.

The arrival of these different racial groups caused a certain amount of friction, but it never became intense as the alien groups were at no time strong enough in numbers to constitute a serious economic threat to the island born population. The contemporary attitude of the white, coloured, and black population towards the Syrian and Asiatic is a mixture of contempt and admiration. Contempt is based on the origin, habits and aloofness of the alien groups. Admiration turns on the fact that they have done so well for themselves. The greatest contempt is reserved for the East Indian who has done least about his position in the society.

Today the whole colour-class system is dependent upon the almost complete acceptance by *each* group of the superiority of the white, and the inferiority of the black.

NOTES AND REFERENCES

1. W. J. Gardner, *History of Jamaica*, London, 1909, p. 172.
2. Ibid., p. 171.
3. Bryan Edwards, *History . . . of the British Colonies in the West Indies*, London, 1801, Third Edition, p. 284.
4. Henry Long, *History of Jamaica*, London, 1774, Vol. II, p. 86.
5. Cf. contemporary U.S.A.
6. Gardner, op. cit., p. 471.
7. H. H. Johnston, *The Negro in the New World*, London, 1910, p. 268.

CHAPTER III

The Contemporary Colour-class System

THE contemporary society in Jamaica does not represent a complete break with the past. Tremendous modifications were inevitable after emancipation but the hierarchical structure was not destroyed. Our pyramidal structure today might look like this:

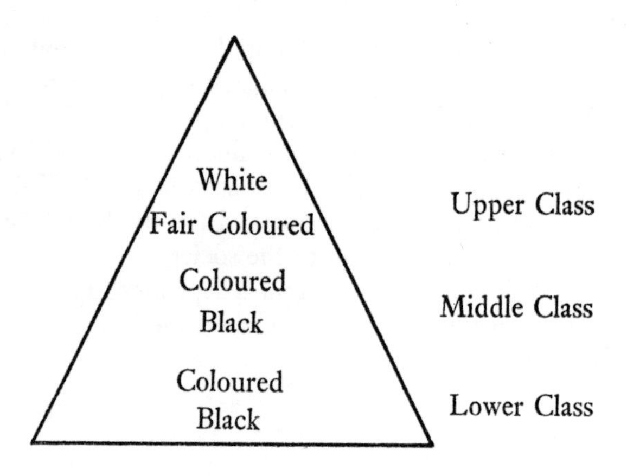

The majority of the black people, who are 78·1 per cent of the total population, can be classified as the labourer-peasant group which we shall term the lower glass.

Government clerkships and elementary supervisory jobs are the preserve of the coloured and black middle class. Shopkeeping and teaching are other professions in which the middle class predominates.

The upper class is composed of whites and fair coloured people who largely monopolize executive positions in the civil service, such occupations as planter, and the professions generally.

This colour-class division is not at all rigid. In the first place, whereas it is useful to indicate economic status, it does not necessarily indicate social position. For example a black doctor is not generally accepted as belonging to the upper class. Again a definite distinction has to be made between the capital, Kingston, the tourist resort of Montego Bay, and the town of Mandeville ('Jamaica's Cheltenham') on the one hand, and the rest of the country on the other. The division made above does not apply to the former places where the white element in the population together with some of the fair coloured, so fair as to be indistinguishable from the European, constitute the upper class. The alien racial groups tend to have class divisions within their own ranks, and to a certain extent they participate in the equivalent class of what we will call the 'native' section of the population.

Differences in this pattern can be observed throughout the Caribbean. The history of the islands has been varied. The successive ownership by French, Spanish, and English, for example in the case of Trinidad, has made the psychology of the people quite different from that of the Barbadian, who has known no other rule save that of Britain. Again the physical size of Barbados as against Jamaica meant that at emancipation there was little or no land for the Negro to settle on; whereas in Jamaica he was able to go to the hills. Such facts would differentiate the Jamaican from the Barbadian. But the all-pervading fact of slavery provides the underlying unity in the Caribbean.

The concept of colour utilized here is one generally current in the West Indies. A coloured man is someone who is of mixed African and European descent. In the United States according to law a coloured man is anyone who possesses any Negro blood whatsoever. This distinction illustrates the whole difference between the colour situation in the British Caribbean and the U.S.A. In the West Indies it is possible for the fair coloured man, if he marries a very fair or white woman, to see his children achieve a higher social status than he has done himself or even possible acceptance by the white group. This is feasible for the American coloured person (in the West Indian sense) only inside his own group. That is if he married a fair person his children might be accepted by a higher social group than his own, but never by the white majority of whatsoever class.

The term black is used to designate those people who are of predominantly African origin. The fair coloured would be that group which, although coloured, is mainly European in appearance.

'Jamaican Whites' and 'Jamaica Red Men' are individuals who although coloured appear like a certain type of blond Englishman after a sojourn in the tropics. These last are indistinguishable from the European except to the eyes of a 'native' observer.

The criteria used by the Jamaicans to evaluate these terms are somewhat complicated. Before attempting an analysis of these it is necessary to discuss what we may call the 'white bias' in the society.

In every colonial society there is both a conscious and an unconscious attitude of ambivalence towards the ruling group. This is composed of subservience and imitation on the one hand, and hatred and repulsion on the other. In the case of a well equipped culture which has been dominated by a European nation (India is an example) there may be what appears to be a complete revulsion against the standards, behaviour, and ideas of the dominant group. E. M. Forster in his novel *A Passage to India* has illustrated the intense conflict in the soul of the Indian. But where much of the aboriginal culture has been destroyed, as was the case of the slave in the West Indies, the feelings of hatred and rejection are very much modified in comparison with the attitudes of respect and imitation. India represents one extreme of this ambivalence, the West Indies the other.

Where a hybrid population is created through concubinage or marriage the conflict is intensified as it now has a physical basis. The mentality of the hybrid is governed by the fact that he may experience rejection from both groups, native and ruler. The Dutch-Javanese are a case in point. The hybrid is more strongly attracted by the dominant group as it offers him more advantages than the native group. He strives for the impossible, that is for complete identity with the white groups. Anglo-Indians and Jamaicans will both speak of an England they have never seen as their 'home'. The degree of isolation of the hybrid varies. In the case of the Anglo-Indian it is almost complete. The society of the Brazilian 'metis' on the other hand is much more integrated.

The coloured person in the West Indies represents a unique phenomenon in the hybrid world. He is generally almost entirely ignorant of African culture and despises what little he does know as being primitive and connected with the undesirable, that is the black. According to his colour he is the prey to much anxiety as to whether he will be able to achieve or has achieved acceptance by the white minority. Even if this ideal is unattainable there is still the conscious anxiety to appear white in his ways and ideas. The intensity of this anxiety varies from individual to individual but is apparent in all.

For such individuals there is a conscious ideal of self-identification with the European or Englishman. However hard he may strive in this direction he can never achieve complete identification as there are the last insurmountable barriers of his tropical environment and lack of personal associations with England. Those that achieve the greatest identification are those who are indistinguishable (from the European observer's point of view) from the European. The dark coloured and black are animated by the same anxieties but to a lesser degree.

It is the writer's opinion that because of the very nature of the material, and because of the colour conscious personality of the individual involved, the European investigator is at a great disadvantage in gathering data. The acute colour consciousness of the West Indian inhibits him from giving information to someone who represents the values he himself is lacking but trying to attain. Some information will be forthcoming, but much of it will be garbled and dressed to suit what the informant thinks are the ideas of the white investigator. This problem is met with in primitive societies but not to the same extent and degree, as the primitive informant does not necessarily feel that information given will affect his social status as so many West Indians do. The same difficulty will be encountered with any coloured group which has been exposed to continuous contact with whites for a long period. It is a criticism which can be applied to Dr K. Little's book, *Negroes in Britain*.(1) The real difficulty lies in the fact that the European is unable to discover whether his material is authentic or not. In the case of the American study *Deep South* this was overcome by having both white and coloured anthropologists engaged in the research.(2)

Perhaps it will help to clarify this discussion if my own position in the colour-class hierarchy is explained.

I am Jamaican born but left the island at an early age and have only maintained intermittent contact since. My parents were both fair coloured people of the upper class, my father being a merchant as was his father before him. My brothers and sisters are all dark but have European-like features and hair. All members of the family rank as upper class (in the sense defined) because of their appearance and the social status of my parents. In this instance dark colouring and European features lead the lower classes to characterize the family as 'coolies'; that is East Indians. My brother, formerly a Resident Magistrate, was called by lower class individuals the 'Coolie Judge'. The family name is one borne by many Jamaica-Jewish families.

Although I belong to the upper class group, my appearance (dark colouring) made it possible for me to be on intimate terms with members of the other classes.

Two attitudes could be discerned towards my inquiries. One was of pleasure and surprise that I was interested in what they thought and said (this was most prominent in interviews at the natal clinics), as it is somewhat exceptional for a member of the upper class to express interest in the lower class. The other attitude was of slight hostility due to my brother's position as a magistrate. This hostility was most apparent during my investigation of Obeah (witchcraft), which is severely penalized by law.

In my opinion the chief reason for my acceptance amongst other colour and class groups was my lack of colour consciousness. This lack of colour consciousness on my part I feel is due to my experience and education in Europe, where the same necessity does not exist for preoccupation with details of colour punctilio in order to ensure one's social position. Many individuals were willing to discuss colour attitudes with me because they felt that although I could be identified as a Jamaican with corresponding sympathies, my long absence had removed me from the Jamaican arena so that they felt that they would not 'lose caste' by saying what they really thought. This was emphasized repeatedly in discussions during which I noticed that the individual would change the topic when another coloured person entered the room.

In other words I had this advantage over the European investigator; I was a Jamaican of an identifiable class, but through the accident of appearance and because of an absence of many years I was able to preserve a detachment, and to be credited because of it as being removed from the mesh of colour relationships.

'Colour' is evaluated in terms of actual colour, hair formation, features, and skin texture. All these are assessed in relation to their nearness to European characteristics and distance from the African. The actual value of a particular characteristic may vary from island to island. For example in Trinidad more emphasis is laid on skin colour than on features, whereas in Jamaica the two are more or less equal.

In Jamaica in order to classify an individual according to colour all the characteristics have to be assessed. It so happens that the majority of the fair coloured have a fair complexion and European hair and features so that their classification is simple. But as regards others it becomes a very complex matter. For instance a person might exhibit European-like features, but his hair might be more negroid than European. In such a case his colour status in the society would be determined by the texture of his skin. This individual would rank above a person of similar complexion with 'good' hair, but whose features were more African.(3) A dark person with 'good' hair and features ranks above a fair person with 'bad' hair and features. There are a very large number of such combinations.

Of the characteristics mentioned two, actual colour and hair, can be artificially treated to produce a 'better' effect.

There are several bleaching creams and lotions, mostly of American origin, on sale in the island. Ordinary peroxide is used as well as a great deal of light face powder. Bleaching creams, etc., have a deleterious effect on the skin and are therefore not much used. Bleaching by artificial means appears to be a practice confined to women. The writer in the course of his field work did not come across a single example of a man using a bleaching material. Dark and black women will, for a festive occasion such as a dance, apply a bleaching lotion, then a type of cream, and finally a mass of white powder. The effect is sometimes grotesque in the extreme. Jamaican fair women are acutely conscious of the slightest possible change in their skin colour. In one case a woman had been sea bathing and so was exposed to the sun. On rejoining friends who had not accompanied her she appeared uneasy in their presence until she said, pointing to her legs, 'The sun was terribly hot today. I must have stayed in it too long, just look at my legs.' In actual fact there was no appreciable difference in the colour of her legs before and after her bathe, but she was afraid there might have been, and to have appeared darker might have affected her position in the group.

Hair straightening, as it is called, is a process by which hair which is kinky or negroid is made to appear more European or straight.

A hairdresser informant stated: 'You would look at her scalp to see if there is any dandruff, then brush it out. Next apply hot oil massaging the hair well which prepares it for a shampoo. You dry the hair leaving a little moisture in it and then apply grease. When the hair is completely dry you start "cultivating" it with a hot comb. You can tell through practice what the hair is like, so you know how much to use the comb. [This comb is made of steel with a wooden handle. It originated in the United States for use amongst the Negro community and was later brought to the West Indies.] Now the hair is all straight. You can use a curling iron on it. Most people like it curled and waved not just straightened, not just dead straight. If it's a small head and the hair is "hard" the treatment will last three to four weeks. If the hair is soft it will last for six weeks or so, or until the person feels it should be done again. Most people seem to do it every two weeks. Once a week is too harassing for the hair. Another thing you have got to be careful about is getting it wet. If you do get wet immediately afterwards, you are liable to catch cold. Later on it doesn't matter about a cold, but if it does get wet it spoils the "straightening" which comes out. Some people won't go in the sea because of this, others don't care and come back and have it done. [In connexion with this another informant said, 'You know it costs these girls 5*s*. every time they have a sea bathe.'] I charge 5*s*. or sometimes they ask me to do it for 3*s*. when they've already washed it at home. There are some people who will charge less than I do but they're no good. Most everybody seems to have it done. Those that you see who don't do it; it's because they have religious reasons or just don't like it, but 75 per cent do it.'

Many lower class women were questioned as to why they had straightened their hair or not as the case might be. These were some typical replies: 'I used to do it, but I won't now, not while I'm having the baby, I might catch cold. But I'll do it again as soon as I've had the baby.' 'I do it but I don't think it's good. You catch cold they say.' 'I don't like it, what God has given you, He knows the reason why. Up to now all my children have good hair, when they grow up they can decide for themselves.' 'I believe in it 'cos it helps make you attractive, but I stopped for a while when I got a cold in the head.'

It appears that generally hair straightening is accepted by lower class women to be an active expression of the feeling that it tends to 'Europeanize' a person. In the upper and middle classes this feeling also exists, although it is not often expressed. Lower class scruples against doing it seem to appear mostly at the time of pregnancy when there is a fear of catching a cold and affecting the health of the unborn child. The fear of catching a cold at any time is also a deterrent. Only a minority appears to have religious scruples regarding its practice.

Some space has been devoted to the practice of 'hair straightening' because its prevalence is an indication of the degree to which the population is affected by a 'white bias'. Another indication is the practice of marrying or co-habiting with a woman of 'better' or lighter colour.

This custom is common to Negro and coloured people everywhere in the New World. Professor Herskovits explains it in terms of an under-privileged minority taking over an outstanding characteristic of the dominant majority, and on the grounds that the lighter coloured Negro with white blood is both socially and economically more favourably situated than his darker brother. (4) Such a hypothesis does not fit West Indian conditions where the Negroes and the coloured people have never been a minority, as occurred in the United States. I am rather inclined to think that, in 'island' terms, both in Jamaica and in the outside world, the knowledge that the Negro is at a disadvantage as against the European has produced in both Negroes and in coloured people a conscious and an unconscious desire to exhibit white traits of all kinds. This has resulted in the deliberate choice of a lighter coloured mate. In this way both a man's colour and that of his children are 'raised', that is the lighter complexion of his mate offsets the bad effects of his own colour in social terms, and his children will be lighter in colour and have greater advantages than if he had married a woman darker than, or the same colour as, himself.

A black peasant proprietor of more than average standing said: 'In the old days the mother of a black or coloured daughter felt a sort of pride in her daughter living with the slave master. "Gone to buckra [master] house, gone live." That feeling still applies. The black girl who cohabits with a white man "Gone lift de color." Mothers would rather their daughters lived with a brown or white man than married a black man.'

A minority opinion amongst the better educated black people was: 'It really hurts me to see my own people behaving in this fashion and refusing to fight back.'

Many lower class women were questioned as to their colour preference in men as husbands or mates. Some typical replies were: 'I prefer darker one, they treat you better.' 'He's darker than me but not so black.' 'I like dark men, they just take my fancy.' 'I like them, they love you and treat you nice.' 'I don't know which I prefer [darker or fairer], it all depends.' 'I like them the same colour.' 'I don't like them too dark, a brown suits me.' 'I like them dark 'cos they're the same as me.' 'The dark ones have "good".'

It is clear from the nature of the evidence forthcoming from lower class women that they support the general tendency in the population for the males to choose fairer mates than themselves. Equivalent evidence of the male preference for fairer mates was also obtained. Similar answers to the above were given, i.e. 'Lighter women are "good" ', etc. An atypical reply was found in the case of a man who preferred darker women because 'That was the way my mother was.' Thus the custom is supported from both the male and the female side. This dual support shows complete psychological acceptance amongst the lower class of the 'white bias'. The two cases quoted earlier are reflections of the slavery attitude when it was essential, if there was to be any improvement in living conditions, for the woman to form a liaison with a white or fair man.

It can be said that the practice of a man 'marrying light' brings prestige to him through the colour of his wife, and to the woman it brings greater economic security because only the more successful men can obtain a fairer mate. It might be thought that women would also attempt to 'marry fair', but this is prevented by the majority of men, particularly the most successful and thus the most desirable as husbands, refusing to take a wife darker than themselves and by so doing losing prestige.

Evidence from the middle and upper classes is very similar to that of the lower class except that its expression is of a more subtle and inhibited character. Ordinary observation of married couples confirms the evidence obtained by interrogation of individual families in all classes. The middle or upper class youth is instructed that a fair wife will greatly improve his chances economically and socially. The young woman is told that a husband not too much darker than herself will be a good match if his economic position is sound.(5)

Another indication of the 'white bias' is the practice amongst well-to-do black or dark families of having servants who are fair. This is done to emphasize to people that although dark they exhibit superiority to most dark people and equality with fair people by employing the latter in a menial capacity. In the island there are some outstanding cases, as that of a wealthy black professional man in the capital who sent to England for a white governess for his daughter.

There appears therefore to be sufficient evidence to say that the society in its class and colour attitudes is motivated by what we have called the 'white bias'.

Colour is not the sole determinant of social position or status. The economic value and prestige value of the individual's employment are factors of considerable importance. Of less importance is the possession of a 'good' family name. In the last thirty years in Jamaica the black man has steadily achieved greater economic opportunity. Recent political events, from 1938 onwards, culminating in the establishment of a practically all-black legislature has given him much greater social prestige than in the past. At the present time the prestige of the black man is probably higher than at any time in the history of the island. In practice this means that there are greater economic opportunities, though not necessarily social ones, open to him. For example in the largest government department the staff, with the exception of the departmental head who is an Englishman, is almost entirely black. This would have been impossible twenty years ago. On the other hand the department most closely associated with executive government is still a preserve of fair individuals, though there is a steady but slight infiltration of people who, by reason of their colour, would not have obtained employment there a decade ago.(6)

The greater economic opportunity presented to the black or dark man has resulted in a change in his psychological outlook. In the past he suffered from a strong sense of inferiority, and a sense that there were things he could not do because he was black, things which only a white or a fair man could do. As in the case of any individual who has been kept in a state of subjection an opportunity to deal with hitherto socially and economically superior individuals on equal or superordinate terms is quickly seized and often abused. To fair people this is merely another example of the inherent inferiority of the black who, when given opportunities, merely abuses them.

It is clear from the foregoing analysis that stereotypes of the different colour gradings exist in everyone's mind. The white has a distinct conception of what the black individual should look like and how he should behave. This is true for all sections of the society. Each colour category has a series of stereotypes for all the other categories, and for itself.

Where the position of a black man is such that he would expect to be admitted to social equality, as for example that of a prominent government official, we may speak of it as public acceptance by, or participation with, the fair group with whom he is in contact. That is to say he will mix with fair people at a public function, and be invited to semi-private entertainments in the homes of fair people. For instance he would be invited to attend a cocktail party given by the *Custos* (the equivalent of the English Lord Lieutenant or American State Governor) of a parish. But he would never be invited to a party to which only close friends consisting of fair people had been invited. Incidentally, *Custos* is one of the offices in Jamaica which has never been held by a black man.

A black man, therefore, cannot become the friend of fair people in the sense of an intimate who is made free of one's house. This tends to produce in black individuals a sense of hostility towards fair people and leads to a kind of social isolation. They feel that black people of an inferior economic status are not sufficiently their equals for them to become intimates. There are ways in which this attitude of fair people can be rendered less rigid. Extreme wealth on the part of the black man, in itself comparatively rare, will lead to a greater degree of acceptance. Of much greater advantage is the possession of a fair or white wife. Then the fair group feels that the wife must be accepted even at the cost of accepting the black husband. But the acceptance achieved by whatever means will never be the same as that extended to fair people of similar economic position.

The reverse of this picture is shown in the treatment meted out to the fair or white people of very low economic status. In Barbados they are known as 'Red Legs'; in the Virgin Islands as 'Cha-Chas'. In Jamaica through the fact that there was a post-emancipation settlement of German peasants in the parish of Westmoreland they are all known, whatever their actual descent, as 'Germans'. There are pockets of them scattered about the island of German, Scottish, and Irish descent. Some have intermarried with black and coloured people, but many, as those in Seaford Town in Westmoreland, have maintained their identity as a white group. Their way of life and their poverty are essentially the same as those of the surrounding black peasant population. The blacks feel that they should exhibit the success and superiority of most white people. White and fair people despise them for letting down their prestige by living like black people. Even if they obtain education and manage to achieve some kind of economic position they continue to carry the stigma of their original status as 'poor whites'.

If other things, such as economic and professional status, are equal, it is colour which is the determining factor in the establishment of social status. This is illustrated by the following case: In a certain town in the island two doctors arrived in succession. One was a Jamaican white who had come to set up in private practice. He was immediately accepted by the upper class group and was invited to their homes. The other was a black man in the government medical service. He was completely ostracized, and his presence hardly noticed by the upper class group.

Behaviour within families of all colours and classes illustrates the depth of colour feeling. If, as often happens, the children in one family are of different shades of colour, the most lightly coloured will be favoured at the expense of the others. From adolescence to marriage the darker members of the family will be kept out of the way when the friends of the fair or fairer members of the family are being entertained. The fair child is regarded as the best asset of the family, and nothing must be put in the way of its success in the form of marriage which will raise the colour status of the next generation. A fair person will try to sever the social relations he may have with darker relatives. Although the rest of the family may at times express resentment at the attitude of the fair members, it generally supports the endeavours of the fair individual to progress socially. In the same way the darker members of a Negro family in the United States will encourage the efforts of a very fair relative to 'pass' for white. The practices of intra-family relations lay the foundation for the public manifestation of colour prejudice.

Colour prejudice is directed much more against dark or black women than it is against similarly coloured men. This may be connected with the fact that there are far fewer means by which women are able to advance economically or professionally. There is a strong prejudice against women in the professions and in the government, which is similar to the attitude which existed in England in the nineteenth century. Professional activity is felt to detract from their womanhood or femininity. The fact that successful black men seek out and marry women of a 'higher' colour in order to improve their social status has led to the creation of a class of well-educated and often well-off black spinsters. These women are unable to get married to the type of man they would like to as such men would wish to marry only women lighter than themselves. The only men available as mates are those belonging to a socially inferior group with whom they will have nothing to do. The result is a group of black women which is prominent in many fields such as education, social welfare and nursing but which is condemned by the strength of the 'white bias' in the society to spinsterhood.

There are very few exceptions to this tendency of educated black women to remain single. One case observed was that of a fair government official who had married a black woman. She had what is known as 'good' features and was prominent in her profession. The couple's friends were mostly dark, but they led a life of comparative retirement, giving as a reason for this that they were both far too busy to entertain. A fair man who marries a dark or black woman ruins his social career. A black man who wishes to be socially successful and who does the same throws away the only opportunity he will ever have of 'raising his colour'.

So far we have discussed colour prejudice as a factor operating in the society on a private level, that is as a factor which determines social distance between individuals in their homes, and in their intimate contacts. Colour prejudice also operates on what we may call the public level.

Institutions on the public level are clubs, hotels, courts, convents, shops, banks, etc.

Most of the big shops and stores in the island, particularly in the capital, are staffed by fair girls. This practice, though still strong, is gradually diminishing. But the very dark or black girl still finds it difficult to get a position of this kind. The rationalization given by the shopowner is on the lines that customers prefer to be served by fair girls. In many stores the 'outside' or counter staff will be fair, and the office staff much darker. The office staff is not, of course, in contact with the public. There is some truth in this rationalization for middle and upper class individuals comment that the fair shop girls 'look so nice'. Some lower class people admit that they like to see fair girls running about at their bidding, but in fact lower class individuals are not always treated with the same courtesy as that which is extended to fair or white people. Another reason for the practice, suggested by shopowners, is that so much of their trade depends on tourists, mainly American, who infinitely prefer being served by fair assistants. This theory is not borne out by the general behaviour of the American tourist in the island, nor does it take into account that many of the prejudices of the American at home undergo a considerable modification abroad.

The tendency towards the employment of fair women in shops is extended to business houses and offices of all kinds. A reason advanced in former days was that there were not sufficient educated dark girls to fill the jobs. This may have been true fifteen or twenty years ago, but it is certainly not true today. Banks, as another avenue of employment, are a monopoly of the fair and light coloured groups. There are four banks with branches throughout the island; one English, and the others Canadian. Many people of all classes and colours who may either approve or disapprove of this 'fair' policy, feel that the banks as 'foreign concerns' are entitled to employ whom they will.

Rationalizations advanced by the different groups do not explain why these practices are tolerated. The fair coloured groups give unqualified acceptance and support to such practices which are quite obviously to their own economic advantage. A small but decreasing uneducated section of the black people support it, saying: 'We could never do what the white people do.' But in most black people the attitude is ambivalent. The black man who condemns such practices outright will himself have married a fair wife.

Lower class comments on 'colour' as a factor in getting a job and in progressing in life are interesting; 'Your colour holds you back, 'cos you hardly see any white people punish, as how coloured people punish.' 'Colour makes a difference in work, some places give preference.' 'Colour affects the job you get.' 'Colour certainly helps as regards a job.' 'If I were fairer I could get a better job.' 'Fair people have a better chance in Jamaica.' 'If you are black you may not get anything to do.' 'If you have a little "cleaner" colour you may get through quicker than the black one.'

Variations of these replies were typical of a cross-section of about 200 lower class individuals. They illustrate the consciousness of black people that their colour is a handicap in the society. They also illustrate the individual's ambivalent attitude towards 'colour', as in most of the cases collected the individual had married a person fairer than himself, and probably also wished to have children fairer than himself.

Legal discrimination on account of colour, class, race, or creed does not exist in the island. There is, however, much discrimination which is supported by public sanction.

Most hotels adopt a policy of discrimination. There is one outstanding exception in one of the largest hotels in the capital which is owned by a Syrian. There everyone is catered for from the American tourist to the black man, but this has only come about in the last ten years.

Many hotels in the island depend to a large extent on the tourist trade which is mainly American. One north coast town caters almost exclusively for tourists. Discrimination is exercised throughout the tourist season from about November to March. Coloured people are met with the excuse, which may be genuine, that no accommodation is available. In the off season they may be made welcome. In any given area prominent black people are usually admitted to public functions at hotels such as dances, but if they are unknown in the neighbourhood they are liable to be excluded. Fair people defend this policy by saying: 'If we don't know them they might be rough black people, and we wouldn't want them here.'

The present racial policy of hotels is largely due to the pressure of political events, and can only be called liberal in comparison to past policies. Since the riots of 1938 and the granting of a new constitution based on universal suffrage, which has resulted in the election of a practically all-black legislature, there has been the beginning of a feeling of pride in being black or dark. This feeling is being continually re-emphasized by the utterances of the political leaders.

Discrimination is not practised in schools. Children of all colours and racial groups attend the same schools. But from an early age the child is able to see the disadvantages of being black as opposed to being fair or white. A Jesuit priest, a teacher, said: 'It's pathetic to see how suddenly a young black boy will realize that the fair boy will have the advantage of him in life. It may be an incident in the playground, or the way someone has spoken to him in the street – sometimes the realization is enough to warp him for life.'

Teachers from England have been known to favour the white and fair children as against the black or dark. The school is the microcosm of the world of colour which awaits the individual outside. There are no rules to favour one group against another, but the approval given to the lighter coloured is as tacit as that given by the society as a whole.

Fair coloured mothers will prevent their children from playing with black or dark children. On being questioned as to why they do this the invariable answer is: 'I don't know where the black child may have come from; with most children of the same colour you know all about them.' There is this much truth in the rationalization

Rose Hall – a ruined Great House from the days of slavery.
Photo: Jamaica Tourist Board

The University Campus at Mona, Jamaica

that most black children do belong to the lower class and so would be undesirable as playmates for a middle or upper class child. But such a remark shows, and it is further indicated by general observation, that fair people associate *all* black people with the lower class.

If the child is not indoctrinated with prejudice by its parents prior to going to school it will mix on perfectly equal terms with children of all colours until some other agency of colour education intervenes.

This is similar to the findings of Bruno Lasker with regard to white and black children in the United States.(7) But there, as in Jamaica, the child is seldom allowed to develop a natural attitude without parental or school interference.

Another agency through which colour prejudice is expressed is the 'lodges'. Jamaica possesses a multiplicity of masonic and quasi-masonic organizations. Some, such as 'Burial and Benefit Societies', exist to serve the practical needs of members. There is, compared with other institutions such as offices and clubs, a marked lack of prejudice exhibited inside particular 'societies'. But a tendency does exist, however, to elect fairer members to high offices though many dark and black people have been prominent in various organizations.

The public expression in newspapers and at meetings of views on colour prejudice is not as frequent as might be imagined from the evidence of strong colour feeling or consciousness. There is in existence a strong sense of constraint against speaking too openly about colour inside a group. Similarly individuals will not do so with members from another group. Thus a fair person would not discuss the position of the black people with a black individual. To discuss such matters in a newspaper or in a public meeting at which all colours may be represented is to offend the Jamaican sense of propriety.

Editorial policy regarding such matters appears to be not to give undue prominence to 'racial' items.(8) On the other hand the activities of 'society' people occupy an extremely prominent position in the daily papers. This means that the activities of white and fair people are reported at great length in the papers the majority of whose readers are black. There seems to be no comment from any group on this anomaly.

One of the leading political parties has been accused of fomenting race hatred in that it claimed Jamaica for the Jamaicans, or Jamaica for the black man. But there has been no great rally to a black banner as against a white or coloured banner. A certain pitch, however, was reached during the riots in 1938 when it was dangerous for white or fair people to venture into the areas of violence as apparently their colour was associated with the government against which people were rioting.

The public utterance by the wife of a highly placed English official, that there was no such thing as colour prejudice in Jamaica, provoked a great deal of comment both in the press and privately.(9) The leading paper adopted a sitting on the fence attitude maintaining that in the sense in which it was made the statement was true, but: . . . 'Differences must be made between national race-prejudice and variations of personal taste. . . . Mrs Ignorant decides that she will not have dark-skinned persons in her drawing-room – the "Pinkman's Club" blackballs brown and black applicants, Miss Black quarrels with her neighbours and finds her climax in "God made Black, God made White, but who made the d. . . . mulatto?" Mr Lillie-White objects to his coloured partner's promotion while Mr Blackman-Rage hates to see a white Jamaican hold any public office and finds it hard to be polite to people fairer skinned than himself, the "Pretty Shop Drapery" will employ only light skinned employees – but none of these things can make Jamaica a colour-prejudice country, even if such attitudes of conduct were general which happily they are not. Mrs Rant, the "Pinkman's Club", Miss Black and her mulatto neighbour, Mr White and Mr Rage, the "Pretty Shop" – may each be prejudiced but the fact remains that Jamaica as such is not colour prejudiced' [*sic*]. The leading article continues to emphasize that there is no prejudice in public life nor before the law, but the practices alluded to in the paragraph quoted are of daily occurrence and affect all sections of the population.(10)

The left wing weekly papers all attacked the original speaker for saying there was no colour prejudice in the island. They in turn were attacked by the chief newspaper in an article which suggested that whenever race was made an issue in Jamaica it was the work of the communists. As it happens there is no communist party in the island.(11)

The whole controversy was most instructive as it showed in miniature the whole complexity of the class-colour situation in Jamaica.

The above quotations illustrate that while colour or shade prejudice is not a topic of daily discussion in the press, when some incident occurs as that mentioned above, it acts as a crystallizing agent and the accumulated feeling of individuals endeavours to express itself publicly. It may be added that the fairer the individual, apropos the 'controversy', the more he was inclined to the view there was no prejudice in Jamaica.

Although the riots of 1938 forced the black man into prominence and to the realization that he was of importance in the island, it was not the first manifestation of black consciousness. In the years before 1914 a remarkable black Jamaican appeared before the English speaking people of the New World. His name was Marcus Garvey. His ideas were concerned with transporting the Negro people of the New World back to Africa. He addressed meetings in the United States, England, and the Caribbean. As a result 'Negro Improvement' societies came into being. Garvey, with the money he obtained from subscribers, launched a steamship company, the 'Black Star Line', which was to provide ships for this mass migration to Africa. On one occasion he addressed an audience in a north coast town in Jamaica. The following is an account obtained from an old resident of the town:

'Garvey spoke to a packed audience of some hundreds, mostly black people. He said: "Wouldn't you like to see a black ship coming into this harbour, wouldn't you like to see a black crew on board, wouldn't you like to see black officers, wouldn't you like to see the passengers all black?" This was punctuated by shouts of approval from the audience. He certainly was a man to make an impression on people.'

Garvey, however, was not a good businessman and his projects failed, though he did purchase a small ship which was manned by an all-black crew with the exception of the engineer who was white. Local comment at the time was that the one white man was the cause of failure! In fact at that time there was no black engineer available. But although Garvey may have failed financially and his grandiose ideas evaporated, he had an incalculable effect on the black people of the U.S.A. and the West Indies. So much so that people still speak his name with reverence, and one of the Negro Congressmen in the United States can speak of him in his autobiography in glowing terms: 'Marcus Garvey was one of the greatest mass leaders of all times. He was misunderstood and maligned, but he brought to the Negro people for the first time a sense of pride in being black.'(12)

Garvey exemplified the messianic tendencies which have been so frequently personified in West Indian history. He died in 1926 but his legend still lingers in the memory of the older black people in the

United States and the West Indies. Bedward was another Jamaican messiah who flourished about the same time as Garvey. He, however, merely promised spiritual redemption, and after an abortive attempt to fly to heaven was confined in the local lunatic ayslum where he died.(13) This messianism and kindred movements are symptoms of worldwide incidence amongst peoples who consider themselves inarticulate and oppressed. The resurgence of the oppressed people may take the form of the Ghost Dance of the Plains Indians, or the Vailala Madness in Papua,(14) or the Garvey movement, but in each case the people affected feel that they are suffering and wish to restore their former, and sometimes imagined, way of life.

The current expositors of black consciousness in Jamaica are a group of people who call themselves Ras Tafarites. They appear to have come into existence at the time of the Italo-Ethiopian War. Members claim spiritual communion with all coloured peoples but particularly with the people of Africa, which country they regard as their home. There are scattered groups of them all over the island, but by far the greatest concentration is in the capital where they live on a stretch of waste ground near the railway station. The men grow beards and in general neglect their physical appearance. Their poverty is extreme. It is interesting to note that at the time of the Ethiopian War popular songs about Haile Selassie were current in both Trinidad and Jamaica.

It has been seen that Jamaican society has as one of its main activating features what we have termed a 'white bias'. This 'white bias' is dependent upon the practices and behaviour of individuals who are both consciously and unconsciously striving to 'lighten' themselves. In their minds black is associated with the backward, primitive and undesirable qualities in man; and white is associated with everything that is desirable. Because of his inescapable colour heritage the mind of the Jamaican is the seat of a deep conflict which is exhibited in the formation of a particular personality configuration. The individual can have little pride of race in himself if he has the appearance of a coloured or black man, and at the same time has the perpetual desire to identify himself with the white man.

The distinction must be made between a coloured and black group which is in the main *legally* as well as socially subjugated, as in the United States, and which produces its own patterns of behaviour; and a society where the majority of the population is coloured and black and is held, partly by its own consent, in a purely social subjection by a white and fair group, which is what occurs in the Caribbean.

The contemporary Jamaican exists in the latter conditions. They are conditions in which he has lost the greater part of the culture of his ancestors. But although he is unable to take over white ideas and culture completely, he can still achieve some measure of identification if his physical appearance allows it. It is this essential in-betweenness, or half-identification, which is the basis of his personality.

The emergence of a more stable type is dependent on a variety of factors. One solution of the problem, that achieved by identification with the 'native' group, has been shown to be doubtful by recent events in the East Indies where the Dutch Javanese are now attempting to establish a separate segregated society of their own. The problem is of a very different nature in the Caribbean. The Jamaican people do not possess any cultural tradition which in their eyes would weigh against the values of the European society as envisaged by them. Until such a tradition develops the 'white bias', together with the personality it involves, will remain a fundamental aspect of Caribbean life.

The ultimate solution lies perhaps in the attitudes adopted in Brazil. In that country society is integrated by the idealization of the 'mixed blood', which, it is emphasized, is the desirable type in the society.(15) Education is capable of doing a great deal in this respect, but much of the good work which it does is nullified by the distortions caused by the necessity of continued European contact.

NOTES AND REFERENCES

1. K. L. Little, *Negroes in Britain*, London, 1948.
2. A. Davis, B. B. Gardner and Mary R. Gardner, *Deep South*, Chicago, 1941.
3. 'Good' connotes European, 'bad' the African.
4. M. J. Herskovits, *The Myth of the Negro Past*, N.Y., 1941, pp. 125–6.
5. Cf. Herskovits, op. cit., pp. 125–6.
6. E.g. no black girls were ever appointed as secretaries to white individuals.
7. Bruno Lasker, *Race Prejudice in Children*, N.Y., 1929. See also K. B. Clark, *Prejudice and Your Child*, Boston, 1963, Chapter I, pp. 17–24.

8. The reverse of this policy is characteristic of Negro-American newspapers.
9. *Public Opinion*, Jamaica, 30.9.46.
10. *Daily Gleaner*, Jamaica, 9.10.46.
11. Ibid., 15.11.46.
12. A. C. Powell, *Marching Blacks*, N.Y., 1945, p. 58.
13. Martha Beckwith, *Black Roadways*, Chapel Hill, 1929, pp. 167–71.
14. J. Mooney, 'The Ghost Dance Religion', 14th Annual Report, 1892–3, Pt. 2, American Bureau of Ethnology, Washington, 1896, and F. E. Williams, 'The Vailala Madness in Retrospect', in *Essays Presented to C. G. Seligman*, London, 1934.
15. D. Pierson, *Negroes in Brazil*, Chicago, 1942, pp. 136–7. See also Gilberto Freyre, *The Racial Factor in Contemporary Politics*, Sussex, 1966.

CHAPTER IV

The Area

As Port Antonio and Portland were the chief centre of my researches I feel that a description of the parish and life in the town is appropriate at this stage of the analysis.

The parish of Portland is in the north-eastern corner of Jamaica. According to the government census of 1943 it has a population of 60,712. The terrain is extremely mountainous, but the soil is very fertile. During the 1914 war the parish had become the greatest banana producing area in the island. But the ravages of Panama and Leaf Spot diseases had a disastrous effect on the bananas, and thousands of acres went out of cultivation.(1) Portland has never really recovered from the effects of this outbreak though bananas are still produced in considerable quantities. Leaf spot can be controlled by spraying, and the government lends a certain amount of assistance in this. Panama disease is far more difficult to control, and the most ruthless methods are necessary such as the complete destruction of trees.

Port Antonio with a population of 6,000 is the chief town of the parish. It is situated between two harbours. The peninsula dividing the latter is known as the 'Hill', and it is the residential part of the town for the upper and middle classes. In the heyday of banana production the headquarters of the three main fruit companies were located in the town. The great majority of the banana plantations in the parish were owned by these three fruit companies, which were American. The 'Hill', dominated by a large tourist hotel, became the enclave of the whites. No ostensible coloured or black person was allowed entry there unless he or she came in a menial capacity. But the American domination of the fruit trade meant prosperity for the workers. Pay, if not good, was adequate. The local hospital was maintained by funds of the companies and employees were treated free. The memory of those days is still cherished by the inhabitants, and this helps to explain the lack of initiative in dealing with the present. Those to whom it is still a living memory tell the younger generation about the spaciousness and glory of former times. As one old man told the writer: 'If you stood on the "Hill" overlooking the West Harbour you'd see as many as twenty ships lying at anchor. In those days they only ran to a few hundreds of tons, so there were a lot of them, American, British, Norwegian, South American. It's very different now, with maybe a ship a fortnight.'

This prosperity was based not only on the fruit trade but also on the advent of tourists and sailors. Port Antonio became the premier tourist resort of the island. American ships made it their first port of call in Jamaica. Tourists would stay at the hotels on the 'Hill', and later travel overland to Kingston, the capital, where their ship awaited them. Sailors from the tourist and banana boats found the town attractive. It is said today that the number of taverns, which is very great for so small a town, is a result of the tremendous liquor trade fostered by the sailors.

Panama disease destroyed all this. Shortly after the 1914 war the fruit companies transferred their head offices to Kingston and began to sell out their plantations in Portland. The population has never quite recovered from this blow. The psychological atmosphere is almost as if the people expected the companies to return one day in the future. Banana cultivation did not entirely cease, it was carried on by the small settler or peasant proprietor who in most cases has taken the place of the company operated plantation. But the yield per acre is very diminished. As the official of a company which still maintains a branch office in Port Antonio said, 'Through disease one acre in Portland is equal to half an acre elsewhere. In St Catherine on company irrigated lands the yield is equal to 200 count bunches an acre, in Portland you get about 40 counts.' (A count bunch is a stem of bananas. There is an average of one stem to a tree.)

Along the coast some landowners have started coconut production instead of bananas, but coconut trees are the major victims of the scourge of the whole north coast – the hurricane. These tremendous winds occur on the average about once every four years. Their force is sufficient to destroy houses and vegetation alike. Of all the parishes in the island Portland is the greatest sufferer in this respect. The hurricane has a psychological effect too. People are disinclined to build a better type of house or have a more careful cultivation as everything may be destroyed in one morning. This attitude together with the memory of the benevolent paternalism of the fruit companies has produced the *dolce far niente* attitude of most Portlanders.

But what neither hurricane nor fruit company can take away is the fertility of the soil. Yet this is not entirely an unmixed blessing. The owner of a plantation showed me a field lying just outside the window of his house and said, 'You see that field. There is every conceivable fruit and vegetable in the West Indies growing there, and do I have to do anything to them? No, I just stick them in the ground and they grow. That's what's the matter with the people of Portland, the soil is too good for them. They're all lazy. Look, I import labour from a hard parish like St Elizabeth where they have to fight the soil to grow anything, and they work marvellously until the Portlanders corrupt them.' There is this much truth in the contention that the Portlander has such an easy time with his land that he is always amazed to learn of mulching, a process of manuring, from migrants from 'hard' parishes.

Government has to a certain extent taken over the role of the fruit companies by the creation of land settlements and the provision of employment in the form of public works. But the contention of the people is that this is not sufficient and more should be done for them. Their political leaders remonstrate with them that they should make a greater effort for themselves, but the attitude still persists.

The story of Port Antonio is the story of all the north coast ports which have known their day of sugar and bananas and have now declined.

The contemporary scene is one of decay as compared with the past. The fruit companies still maintain branch offices in the town but they are merely buying agencies. Bananas are still loaded in the West Harbour but in far fewer numbers. The 'Hill' remains as a residential area, but it is no longer a white enclave, and there are even a few black working folk living there. The chief hotel was destroyed by fire and hurricane, though the annexe remains to cater not only for white tourists but for islanders as well. The great company plantations have almost disappeared. Many have been bought by the government and turned into land settlements for small peasant proprietors, as have those surrounding the town. Others are still in private hands or have been sold piecemeal. All the activities of the past go on but on a very much diminished scale.

The stratification of the society is that described in Chapter II. The black or lower class people form the greatest part of the population of the town. They comprise peasants, that is people who get their living solely from the land, wharf labourers, general labourers, domestic servants, a few craftsmen such as bootmakers, shop assistants, and the unemployed.

Those classified as peasants may vary from the individual with one or two acres to the real peasant proprietor with several acres, who may be admitted as a member of the middle class. But the black lower class man or woman in the town never really loses connexion with the land whatever his or her occupation may be. Practically every house in the town has a strip of ground in which something edible is grown. Some families may have a field in the hills nearby which they cultivate whenever there is time to spare from other occupations. Exception must be made of the unemployed who are often quite destitute. There is also a distinction between the peasant who has his piece of land in the hills where he lives and works, and the peasant on land settlement. Holdings on a land settlement can be bought with government aid over a period of time. Government Agricultural Banks help towards the purchasing of land on a settlement. But the peasants' criticism is that they can only borrow money if their credit is good, and that if their credit were good they would not want to borrow money from the government, so that they get no assistance in any case.

Holdings vary from one to about fifteen acres, most of them being about five acres. There has been much argument in Jamaica recently over the desire of the black people to get away from the land. The great increase in the unemployed in the capital which is due to migration from the country parts appears to show that the black people are tending to leave the land. On the other hand, all the claims were taken up on a land settlement near Port Antonio on the very day that it was thrown open to the people. The truth seems to be that while a section of the population, mostly those under twenty-five, is attracted by other avenues of employment, there is an equally large section which is determined not to leave the land. In conversations with farm workers returned from the United States the desire to obtain a piece of land was a constant motif. Many of these farm workers had even sent home money from the States in order to purchase land which they could work when they returned.

Bananas are the staple cash crop. The grower contracts with one of the three companies to supply a certain amount per week throughout the year. His contract does not prevent him from selling to another agency if he wishes to do so, but generally the contract is kept. During and since the war the government has used the companies as buying agencies. The price to the grower was fixed in 1947 at 7*s*. a count bunch – that is a full stem obtained from a single tree. During the war there was a period when no bananas were exported from Jamaica at all, but the government continued to buy to save the growers from extinction. One of the companies was a co-operative organization but it was forced by competition to change its composition, and it is now on a more or less quasi-co-operative basis.(2)

These companies will accept contracts from growers with as little as one acre under cultivation, though the average size of a holding is about three to five acres. Although there are big company plantations in such parishes as St Catherine's, in Portland and in the majority of the fourteen parishes in the island the banana is now a small settler's crop.

In Portland the banana suckers – the young plants – are planted about eleven feet apart and eighteen inches deep in earth which has been forked. The only attention required after that is a little forking from time to time to keep the soil loose round the young trees. During the year the trees send out suckers which are cut off and replanted where necessary. The average yield is two crops a year. In very good disease-free soil it is possible to get as many as three or four crops a year. The slackest period for buying appears to be from Christmas until March.

The grower must bear the cost of carting his bananas from his holding to the wharf in the town. This cost varies from 6*d*. a bunch for a distance of 12 miles, to 9*d*. a bunch for 15 miles.

The night before a ship is loaded the town is filled with the noise of lorries carrying bananas to the wharf from the outlying districts. There is an air of general excitement as everyone knows that money is coming into the town.

As well as bananas the peasant grows a variety of food crops such as yams, dasheens, cocoes, and yampies. These are all carbohydrate root crops, and are the commonest article of diet for the Jamaican. The yam is planted in October and bears in September. It is planted in forked ground and a bank is built up over the roots. The head of the largest root is cut off and replanted, which practice maintains a constant supply of roots for planting. The saying is, 'Every time it bears use the head.'

Such crops can be marketed through the government which maintains a buying department in Port Antonio, and sends round a lorry to the outlying districts once a fortnight to buy and collect produce. The produce is sent on to the capital and sold in the large markets there. The grower is not compelled to sell to government, he may sell to a 'higgler'. These are generally women who find it a very satisfactory occupation as it gives them the maximum of independence. They travel around the countryside buying and transporting the produce to the best market which is often that of the capital. There would appear to be very little profit in the transactions as they have to pay the rail fare to Kingston and the cost of somewhere to sleep when they are there. However, it is an occupation which gives them full scope for the Jamaican habit of long conversations about nothing in particular, and they are no one's servant.

The higgler may keep a shop in the town where she sells the produce bought in the country, or she may practise door to door selling all over the district. The grower may do this himself or get his 'wife' or children to do it for him. Every morning on the 'Hill' the air is filled with the cries of the different sellers of vegetables, fruits, and fish.

The fourth and most important method by which the peasant may dispose of his produce is through the local market.

The market is situated in the centre of Port Antonio. It is a very simple structure of stone pillars supporting a corrugated iron roof. This is surrounded by a low wall surmounted by tall iron railings. Inside are some stalls as for example in the meat section, but the majority of sellers display their wares on the floor which is of stone. Space may be rented from sixpence to over a shilling for a large pitch. Market day is Saturday, and from Thursday evening sellers begin to arrive. The local government authority has erected a shelter for these people which costs a penny a night, but many prefer to sleep out in the open and are to be found sleeping in the streets adjacent to the market.

A little selling is done on Fridays but not much. By Saturday morning the market is in full swing and the building is crowded with both buyers and sellers. A local official called the clerk of the market is in charge of the operations – he is kept fully employed as there are constant disputes.

The market has the obvious function of facilitating the exchange of produce and money between individuals. But it has another and equally important function. It enables the Jamaican to meet his friends and relatives in an atmosphere of bustle and excitement which is enjoyed by everyone. Women of all classes meet in a friendly atmosphere so that in one sense the market acts as a binding force for the whole society.

Friendships can be renewed and gossip exchanged. Members of kin groups are brought into contact with each other. There is a party atmosphere in the evenings when the day's selling is done and there is a pause before they begin what may be a long trek back home. This is a point to be emphasized; many sellers may come from districts which although near the town in terms of mileage may be quite unaccessible due to the the nature of the terrain. To these the weekly market day is perhaps the only time they leave their mountain villages and come in contact with people from outside their settlements.

It is noticeable that by far the great majority, over 80 per cent of the buyers and sellers in the market, is women. The only really male occupation is that of meat selling. Children are very much in evidence at all times in the market. Very often they fall asleep in the mothers' arms as animated gossip is carried on into the night. For the Jamaican the market is business centre, theatre, forum, and party all in one.

The unemployed forms a large minority of the lower class. A section of them may obtain casual work as banana loaders, but this is dependent upon the arrival of ships which occurs about once a fortnight. But the majority is almost entirely destitute. They depend for existence on alms, on an occasional odd job, or on the great stand-by, 'relief works'. Relief works are works sponsored by the central or local government. They include road building and maintenance. Such work is not always necessary but has to be projected in order to meet the needs of the unemployed. At the approach of a holiday period such as Christmas or Easter the people demand that work be given them in order that they shall have some 'Christmas' or 'Easter' money. The wage is 6*s*. a day with a maximum of four days' work in any given week. This dependence on government to provide a means of employment is characteristic of the Portlander's attitude of waiting for something to happen.

The entire blame for the attitude of dependence cannot be placed on the memory of the paternalism of the fruit companies as it is a phenomenon found all over Jamaica in areas where the fruit companies did not operate. It may be due in part to the excessive starch content of the normal diet which tends to produce a definite physical lethargy.

Assessment of income provides a very difficult problem in the lower class. The labourer in most cases ekes out his wages by selling his produce, though part of the produce will be consumed by the household. It is impossible to assess this on a cash basis. However, the 1943 census gives the following figures: of a total of 79,006 people in the island engaged in domestic service of whom 67,607 were women, over 25 per cent were earning less than 6*s*. a week; 25 per cent were unpaid (meaning that they were children falling into the category of 'schoolgirls' described below); and approximately 12 per cent earned between 10*s*. and £1 a week. Of 55,874 labourers, 12,416 of which were women, approximately 25 per cent earned less than 10*s*. a week, and approximately 25 per cent earned under £1 a week. Of those classified as engaged in agricultural labour (those working as hired labour on someone else's land) totalling 124,354, of whom 31,498 were women, approximately 17 per cent were classified as unpaid (working for relatives), approximately 12½ per cent earned under £1 a week, and approximately 33 per cent under 10*s*. a week.

The unemployed in the three categories mentioned: domestic servants, general labourers, agricultural labourers, numbered approximately 16 per cent, 60½ per cent and 25 per cent respectively in the week that this particular census of wage earners was taken.(3)

Poverty naturally affects the type of housing. This is in addition to the fact that even if people do have the money they may not spend it on improving their house and property because of the fear of hurricanes. Housing tends to improve on the land settlements under indirect government supervision. But the houses of the lower class in the town proper and the surrounding districts tend, with few exceptions, to be simple one storey structures of wood and corrugated iron.(4) In one district near the town government has started to erect new houses for the workers, but peasant criticism is that they are too small for their families. Observation confirms this.

Increased income in the middle class does not necessarily lead to improved housing. Houses tend to be bigger, but the same materials are used. Variation may be the substitution of cedar tiles instead of zinc for roofing. There may also be more facilities, such as a bathroom or a wash-house. But the general appearance is poor.

Housing in the upper class is by no means correlated with income. Houses are slightly more spacious than those of the middle class but with few exceptions the furnishings are austere. The writer noticed that in planters' homes all over the island there was very little display of wealth. In a comparative group in England, the upper middle class, there is a much greater display of wealth. This practice of limiting the display of wealth is in complete antithesis to the behaviour of the eighteenth and early nineteenth century planters.

A characteristic of people of all classes, which is not affected by income, is their extreme hospitality towards each other and towards strangers. The poorest home will always manage to produce some refreshment for the visitor, and only at the risk of insulting his host can he refuse it. The slightest pretext of an introduction will ensure a welcome from members of any class.

Topographically the arrangement of the town is simple. The peninsula of the 'Hill' divides to two harbours. At the extremity is the eighteenth century fort which has been converted into the main elementary and secondary school for Port Antonio. In the same grounds is the tennis club of the upper class. Living on the 'Hill' are upper and middle class people with, in recent years, a sprinkling of the lower class. Where the peninsula joins the mainland at the foot of the 'Hill' is the centre of the town which is focused round the Court House. Two main roads meet here. The road to the west is the shopping centre. Most of the shopowners live here over their premises. As this road tails off into a land settlement in the west houses are interspersed between shops. The road to the east is lined by a few shops and then develops into the middle class residential area, with by-roads leading to the sea. Two land settlements are to be found at the end of this road. The land settlements are about a mile and a half from the centre of the town. The lower class area is between the arms of the east and west roads. The Anglican church, a prominent building, is a quarter of a mile from the Court House on the east road. A turning a hundred yards or so from the centre of the town on the west road leads up a steep winding road to the hospital which, from its eminent position, dominates the working class area and almost the whole of the town.

It is important to realize the proximity of the land settlements to Port Antonio. This means that most of the townspeople are in intimate contact with the soil, and however 'urbanized' they may become, never quite lose their affinity with the peasant. This process is reinforced by the fact that a large section of those engaged as labourers either keep a cultivation at home or up in the 'bush'.

The Jamaican is very keen on changing his domicile and work. As regards the upper and middle classes the government fosters this tendency by its policy of switching officials from place to place at comparatively short intervals. The lower class Jamaican is not dependent on government to assist him in this way. He goes from parish to parish seeking work. The seasonal employment of sugar estates tends to increase the process. There are no figures available for Port Antonio, but the census states that 79·9 per cent of the population in Portland was resident in its place of birth on the day that this particular census was taken. This appears to be about the average for the island. The equivalent figure for Kingston is given as 64·4 per cent which bears out the impression that there is a constant change-over in the composition of Jamaican urban dwellers as exemplified by Port Antonio.

Upper class amusements are mainly confined to the activities of the tennis club which sponsors not only tennis but bridge and dances from time to time. Considerable opposition is aroused in the town when the club attempts to raise funds by dances for which middle class people are invited to buy tickets, because on other occasions a rigidly exclusive policy is maintained. Bridge parties take place in private homes, and occasionally picnics are arranged either in the country or on privately owned estates near the town.

The middle class had their own club, but it was destroyed by fire some years ago and has never been rebuilt. Visiting appears to take the place of bridge in this class. A little poker is played by men in shop rooms, and the illegal Chinese gambling game of Peako Peow is also played. This is similar to the American 'numbers' game.

The cinema is a focus of amusement for all classes. There is only one cinema in the town which shows a different film every other day including Sundays. Inside the cinema there is a class stratification based on price. The lower class occupies the cheapest seats which cost 9*d*., and the upper class the most expensive at 2*s*. 6*d*., with the middle class in between. When all the cheapest seats are full, members of the lower class are allowed to bring in their own chairs which they place in the side aisles. Behaviour in the cinema is extremely appreciative; films are followed with an accompaniment of sighs and grunts of approval. Before the showing of a film the national anthem is played. During the author's stay in the town it was the practice of the lower class, while all the middle and upper class people stood rigidly to attention, to continue to sit laughing and shouting as they had been doing before the anthem. This led to complaints by the upper class. A notice was then flashed on the screen which asked patrons to stand up and keep quiet during the national anthem, but if they did not wish to do so would they kindly leave the cinema while it was played and return afterwards.(5) It was also observed that when Africans were portrayed on the screen the immediate response was laughter. American Negroes provoked laughter and approval. The cinema is a major influence in the lives of people. To many it represents the only way of overcoming the unbearable monotony of a cramped home to which the only other alternative is the street.(6)

Dominoes is another major amusement of the lower class. It is played by men in the fronts of shops after closing time and outside houses. Two players attract a considerable crowd. The game is played with a great banging of pieces on the table as moves are made.

Dances in the Town Hall or Court House and the Market are patronized by both middle and lower class people. Here are to be seen the latest 'zoot suit' fashions from the United States. These consist of very baggy trousers with extremely narrow bottoms which almost enclose the foot just above the shoe. Shirts of lurid colours are worn under coats reaching nearly to the knee. To offset the whole ensemble a gold or silver key chain is looped obtrusively outside the trousers. This fashion was brought back from the States by returning Jamaican farm workers and seems to be the ideal of all lower class men.

A club for the lower class has been formed on one of the land settlements. It has a small pavilion where impromptu dances can take place, together with a field for playing football and hockey. The venture has proved quite popular, and other clubs are in the process of formation.

At Christmas time what is known as 'Coney Island' comes to Port Antonio. This is a sort of travelling show with stalls where fair games can be played. It is like a miniature Hampstead Heath on Bank Holiday and lasts for some weeks. Music is provided by drummers though there is no dancing. It produces a brilliantly lit little area by the wharfside.

Another Christmas manifestation on Christmas and Boxing Day is the Mummers or John Canoe Dancers. They seem to have had their origin in the dances given by the slaves in front of the 'Great House' of the sugar estates on Christmas morning. The dancers consist of a troupe of about six men with drummers wearing fancy dress. Some are dressed as women. They enact stories which may be of African or European origin. The participants themselves are quite unaware as to their content or meaning, but say: 'We've always danced like that.' One dancer is dressed as a Red Indian, another as a Princess, and John Canoe himself wears a tent shaped costume covered with feathers, cloth and bits of mirror. The mummers are the delight of children who follow them from house to house as they perform, and collect money from their audience. John Canoe is said to have been a famous personage on the Gold Coast in the eighteenth century, but his real origin is obscure. Martha Beckwith gives an interesting account of him in *Black Roadways* (Chapel Hill, 1929, pp. 149–56).

In the sphere of religion Port Antonio is representative of the parish. Jamaica as a whole possesses examples of most of the religious organizations to be found in Europe and America. The table on page 83 from the 1943 census shows the percentage distribution in Jamaica of the more important religious groups.

As is to be expected the bulk of the membership of practically all the religious groups is composed of black people. In Portland out of a population of 60,712, roughly 42 per cent belong to the Anglican Church, 26 per cent to the Baptist, 9 per cent to the Methodist, 1¼ per cent to the Adventists, 1½ per cent to the Quakers, and 1 per cent to the Roman Catholic Church. The Anglican and Roman Catholic churches carry a higher prestige value than the other groups. The great majority of upper class people in the town are either Anglican or Roman Catholic.

The rites of the orthodox churches are similar in detail to those of the parent bodies in Europe or elsewhere. These churches make no attempt in ritual, or in the conduct of the services to satisfy the emotional needs of the majority of the people. But organized religion in the form of the orthodox churches does, however, serve an extremely important social end. It was suggested earlier that the market acts as a binding force in the society. A church has a similar function. Here the upper and middle class men and women meet not only each other but members of the lower class as well. The orthodox churches are a powerful factor making for solidarity. The buyer–seller relationship has no place here, but the church is the only place in the society where colour-class attitudes do not profoundly affect inter-personal relationships. However, this is true only of the orthodox churches; the membership of the 'native' or cult bodies is exclusively composed of the black lower class.

Attendance at an orthodox church brings into prominence another characteristic of the lower class Jamaican. Lack of decent clothing will prevent attendance. Those who attend wear their best clothes. In the same way in the Law Courts no man will be admitted without a jacket, or a woman without a hat. Those who are extremely religious but who lack means to provide themselves with adequate clothes will

TABLE 1

Religious denomination	*Per cent of all religious groups*
ALL RELIGIOUS GROUPS	100·0
Anglican	28·3
Baptist	25·8
Methodist	8·9
Presbyterian	7·5
Roman Catholic	5·7
Moravian	4·1
No religion	4·0
Church of God	3·5
Adventist	2·2
Congregationalist	1·7
Non-denominational	1·6
Salvation Army	1·1
Christian	0·5
Brethren	0·4
Evangelical Association	0·4
Pentecostal	0·4
Friends	0·3
Hindu	0·3
Plymouth Brethren	0·3
Pocomania	0·3
Bible Student	0·1
Jewish	0·1
Mission	0·1
Bedwardite	*
Christian Science	*
Buddhist	*
Confucian	2·1
Not specified	0·3

* denotes a very small percentage.

gather outside the church during a service, but will go away before the congregation comes out. Shoes are rare amongst the lower class, but great efforts are made to obtain a pair to wear on Sundays. In order to avoid dirt and wear an individual often carries his shoes until he is near the church when he puts them on.

It will be seen that churchgoing is in fact regarded by most people as a means of demonstrating their status in the society. To appear in the congregation badly dressed is to admit lack of respectability.

The 'native', as opposed to the orthodox religious groups, rely entirely on lower class support, and are served by a black 'clergy'. In origin they may be either specifically Jamaican, as in the case of the Bedwardites, or American, as the 'Church of God'. In ritual they approximate more to the cult groups than the orthodox churches. But obviously with their restricted class membership they do not serve the function of creating social solidarity as do the orthodox bodies.

The cult groups serve a somewhat different purpose. Their membership is exclusively black. There is no desire on the part of the congregation to demonstrate status through clothing. But on the other hand they do cater to the desire for emotional stimulation and excitement which is prevalent in the lower class throughout Jamaica. This desire and its partial gratification in a religious form must be seen against the background of extreme poverty and lack of social opportunity. The cult groups provide the means of temporary escape from the tedium of everyday life.

Pocomania is the most prominent of these cult groups. The estimate of 0·3 per cent in the census table is, in the opinion of the writer, a serious underrating of its actual strength. As all cult group activity is strongly condemned by the upper and middle classes it is probable that many individuals are reluctant to admit their connexion with Pocomania. The attendance at 'meeting houses' in Portland suggests a substantial support from the lower class. Many adherents are, however, sporadic in their attendance, others belong to the 'native' or orthodox churches as well as being Pocomania devotees.

Throughout the island in every district there is a cult leader who represents the desire of the people to produce miraculous things without the assistance of the machinery of everyday living, and in defiance of the government. Then also to become a cult leader enables the individual to exercise power over people, and at the same time it serves to increase his income through paid consultations, while the group feels that the leader is expressing its desires for power and prestige, and simultaneously the individual is able to crystallize in himself the group feeling. In general the social situation of poverty and frustration facilitates the development of such feelings and attitudes.

Pocomania can be described as a type of Christian revivalism combined with certain specific West African religious devices, such as the use of the trance. Its origin can possibly be traced back to the Myal movement of slavery days. Myal was a quasi-religious movement of the slaves which was directed against practitioners of witchcraft, the Obeahmen. The function of the Myal man or leader seems to have been to combat the evil forces of Obeah. For this purpose a dance was utilized and the dead person (the person obeahed) was anointed with a herbal decoction and restored to life. Certain herbs were employed which were said to induce a trance-like state. The opposition between a Myal leader and an Obeahman was not always clear, as often the former would uncover and destroy Obeah which he himself had created and buried. The modern descendants of the Myal men, the Pocomanians, induce trances by autosuggestion during which they are supposed to receive the 'spirits', and to talk in 'tongues'.(7)

The last great outbreak of Myalism was in 1842. After that it seems to have coalesced into various forms of revivalism which have always been current in Jamaica since the introduction of Christianity to the mass of the people. The appeal of revivalism to a people who were deprived of normal channels of expression even after emancipation is clear.

Pocomania is essentially a proletarian movement. It is publicly practised. In its group activity the individual can feel identification with something which is greater than himself. This identification acts as a form of compensation for the general ills of life which affect everybody. Here it is in direct contrast to Obeah, which purports to satisfy the desires and remove the ills of the individual as opposed to the group. Obeah is secret; Pocomania is public.

These are the fundamental differences: Pocomania is an institution operating at the level of the group which unifies the lower class element of Jamaican society, and is feared and condemned by the other classes; Obeah is clandestine, is dominant in intra-personal relationships, and disturbs the harmony of the group. It is significant that whereas Pocomania is confined to the lower class, Obeah adherents are found at all class levels.

Despite the very real distinction, however, there are certain similarities. Both institutions appear to have their origin in the West African conception of witchcraft (Obeah), and a form of white magic (Myal). Both take their leaders from the lower class. And for the lower class individual Obeah and Pocomania offer opportunities of leadership and self-expression which are denied him by the greater society. One has a Christian basis, and the other, Obeah, possesses elements of both Christianity and West African magic. It must be noted that the personnel of the leader section of both movements may be, and often is, interchangeable.

In Port Antonio there are several meeting houses where the rites and ceremonies of the Pocomanians are characterized by an enthusiasm and verve not to be found in the orthodox churches. Obeah has its secret practitioners who can always be found when necessary. Every chemist is reputed to be an Obeahman, or to be able to obtain the assistance of one. In the incidence of Pocomania and Obeah both the town and the parish are typical of the island.

When there is nothing else to do, and he has no money, the lower class Jamaican can always attend a religious meeting in the street. In Port Antonio there is usually one every night and several at week-ends. These vary from the Salvation Army to Methodists and travelling Pocomania preachers. If all else fails there is still the major delight of all Jamaicans, conversation. There is always time for the Jamaican to enjoy conversation no matter what hour of the day or night it may be. He has learned through experience that the greatest amusement comes from the discussion of everything under the sun. In the evenings little knots of people will be seen throughout the town busily discussing not only issues of government and rent, but also more profound metaphysical problems.

In Port Antonio law and order is represented by the magistrate in his court and by the police. Magistrates are known in the island as judges, and are equivalent to the London police court magistrates. The actual enforcement of the law depends on the character of the individual holding the office. The people are very quick to sense whether he is a 'strong' man and so liable to give them what they call a 'bad' time. Before the arrival of a certain judge in 1944 Portland had the reputation of being particularly lawless. This judge was a 'strong' man, and the people feared his sentences. When a rumour was started that he was to be transferred many lower class people were very jubilant. Their jubilance was short-lived, however, as he remained.

The judge holds his chief court in Port Antonio about four times a week. Once a fortnight he visits the chief townships in the parish to hold a court. For lower class people going to court is a major form of entertainment. The court will not allow anyone to enter if they are not properly dressed; women must wear a hat, and men a jacket, so it gives the people an occasion to dress up. The witnesses and their friends wear their very best clothes. Those who do not go into the court congregate outside, and there is always more animation in the town on a court day. To many who attend it means a long journey from remote settlements in the hills, but there is ample recompense for this in the satisfaction of meeting their friends, and of generally enjoying themselves.

Going to court for the Jamaican is not only a form of amusement; as a witness in a civil or criminal case his appearance in court gives him prestige in the society. He becomes the centre of attention and people talk about him. This may help to explain the comparatively high incidence of minor crimes, as even the minor criminal in court seems to enjoy his notoriety. No stigma attaches to an appearance in court, or to a prison sentence. One judge stated that a woman witness in a criminal case was incensed at the suggestion that an individual who had been released from a murder charge on the grounds of some technicality was her lover. This was not because of his presumed homicide, to which she had given no thought, but because he did not 'appeal' to her. An extremely common expression heard all over the town is, 'Mind now, or I tek you to court.'

On the other hand where punishment is inclined to be severe, as in cases of praedial larceny, it is difficult to get peasants to testify against each other. The attitude is: 'They poor people like us.'

There is no doubt that the Jamaican is litigious. Solicitors in Port Antonio say that though many of their clients have the flimsiest of excuses for bringing a case against someone, the clients are disgusted with them if they say that there is not enough evidence to take the case to court. 'I must find me a better laywer.' Typically: a friendly argument in a tavern may develop into a fight; the police arrive; the contestants are arrested; and at the next court day the accused and all their friends appear in court. The issue is debated not only inside the court house, but outside in the streets and taverns.

The court is definitely an avenue of expression for lower class people. What does a small fine or even a few days in gaol matter beside the prestige with which they return to their village or the town?

The punishment for disorderly conduct and indecent language, the most frequent offences before the court, is a fine of £2 or thirty days for the first offence, and £3 or thirty days for a second offence. For assault there is generally a fine of 5*s*. or a few weeks' hard labour.

Praedial larceny is generally punished by the cat-o'-nine-tails, or hard labour for six months, or both. For wounding the punishment is a fine up to £1 or hard labour. Obeah is a serious offence which is extremely difficult to prove. It has a penalty of two years' hard labour. The punishment for growing or smoking ganja is generally six months' hard labour.(8)

The following statistics give an indication of the incidence of crime in the parishes of Portland and Hanover. Hanover is the most westerly parish in the island and Portland is the most easterly. The figures given are for 1939 because the war years with their general unsettling atmosphere and the fact that many people were away from the island in the armed forces or in the United States as farm workers, would not give a true indication of the normal incidence. For comparative use the figures are given for crimes in Portland during 1943.(9)

TABLE 2

Offence	*Portland*		*Hanover*
	1939	1943	1939
Disorderly conduct	217	217	231
Assault	266	339	90
Grave assault	24	33	13
Vagrancy	26	42	17
Larceny	65	299	80
Praedial larceny	26	102	40
Wounding	64	124	40
Indecent language	99	330	150
Rape	—	4	—
Obeah	4	2	1
Ganja (growing or smoking)	8	55	—

NOTES AND REFERENCES

1. The first cases of Panama disease in Jamaica were reported from Portland in 1911–12. 'It has been suggested that the disease was brought to Jamaica on the boots and tools of labourers returning from the infected lands in Central America.' C. W. Wardlaw, *Diseases of the Banana*, London, 1935, p. 15.
2. For an excellent account of the growth of the banana industry, see Lord Olivier, *Jamaica : The Blessed Island*, London, 1946, pp. 377–94.

3. *Report of Jamaica Nutrition Committee*, Jamaica, 1937, gives the average weekly wage of male workers in the island as 14*s*., and states that the average for women was less. The figures for 1960 are approximately 46*s*. a week for men and 30*s*. for women—O. C. Francis, *The People of Modern Jamaica*, Jamaica, 1963, Chapter IX.
4. The housing of the lower class is treated in more detail in the section on the family.
5. Many did leave the cinema and returned afterwards.
6. Taverns are patronized mainly by lower and middle class men; some have a special room reserved for upper class patrons. Rum is the chief drink consumed and can be bought at most grocery stores. There are no licensing hours. Despite the cheapness of rum – a few shillings a bottle – there is little public drunkenness.
7. Martha Beckwith, *Black Roadways*, Chapel Hill, 1929, pp. 142–56, contains a good description of Myalism.
8. Ganja, *Cannabis sativa*, is known more popularly in England and America under its Mexican name, marijuana.
9. The population of Hanover is 51,684, as against 60,712 in Portland (Jamaica Census of 1943). Statistics for Hanover in 1943 were not available. In the 1960 Jamaica Census the population of Portland was given as 63,852, and that of Hanover 53,917.

CHAPTER V

Concubinage and Marriage

THE lasting strength of the promiscuous tradition of slavery can be clearly seen in contemporary Jamaica.

It is necessary to define the terms used in the context of concubinage. Concubinage itself is common law marriage, the union of a man with a woman which lasts indefinitely without the full sanction of law. Limited promiscuity is used to describe the behaviour of a man or a woman who has casual unions with a number of the opposite sex, but who eventually settles down with one only. This behaviour usually occurs when the individual is young. Promiscuity is taken to mean unrestricted sexual freedom. Polygamy describes a man or woman cohabiting with more than one of the opposite sex. All these modes of behaviour are given no recognition by the law, but there is strong social sanction in their favour.

TABLE 3

Year	*Percentage of illegitimate births*
1918	68·5
1926	73·7
1928	71·46
1929	71·47
1930	71·75
1931	71·76
1932	71·71
1933	71·64
1934	71·89
1935	72·23
1936	71·66
1937	71·28
1942	69·93

In the 1943 Census of Jamaica the term illegitimate is used to denote children born outside of legal marriage. The illegitimacy figures for certain years show the strength of concubinage as an institution.

Comparative figures for certain of the other British West Indies show the positive relation which their illegitimacy rates bear to Jamaica. In 1939 Trinidad's illegitimacy rate was 65 per cent, Grenada's in 1940 was 64·2 per cent, British Guiana's in the same year was 48·4 per cent, and Bermuda's in 1941 was 19·08 per cent.(1)

In the following table mothers are classified according to their marital status.(2)

TABLE 4

	Number	*Mothers Per cent*	*Children born Number*	*Children born Per cent*	*Average number of children born*
Total	168,471	100	610,871	100	3·6
Single	60,048	35·6	160,324	26·2	2·7
Married	55,812	33·1	255,058	41·8	4·7
Common law	49,246	29·2	179,586	29·4	3·6
Widowed	3,124	1·9	15,182	2·5	4·9
Divorced	241	0·2	721	0·1	3·0

From this table it can be seen that about 70 per cent of all children are born to women in some form of permanent union.

In Portland in 1942, 27·5 per cent of the population over fifteen was classified as married, in St Thomas the figures were 21·4 per cent, and in St Mary 24·4 per cent. These two parishes are the eastern and western neighbours of Portland. Both are notorious for Obeah practices and appear to exhibit a high degree of social disorganization. Portland is not a sugar parish whereas both the former are. Observation seems to bear out the island contention that in sugar parishes the degree of social disorganization is greater than elsewhere. In assessing the figures given above it should be borne in mind that the majority of the Jamaican population, 78·1 per cent, is black. In Portland the black people constitute 85 per cent of the total, in St Thomas 88·6 per cent, and in St Mary 80·9 per cent.(3)

Conditions tending to the perpetuation of concubinage are varied. The economic factor is of great importance. As has been said previously the average peasant and town dweller live on the poverty line. There is widespread unemployment and bad housing conditions. It is in this framework that the other causes operate.

It cannot be said that there is a rooted antipathy to marriage. Of over 100 women interviewed at the town pre-natal clinic 75 per cent wished to get married, but it appeared that the men were unwilling.

The statements were not volunteered with any animosity against the man in question, but rather in depreciation of a situation of which it was thought the questioner disapproved. A number of men interviewed (20) appeared to be frightened of settling down with one woman. They had a fear of the woman ceasing to work or leaving them. This was corroborated by other interviews where men stated that concubines demanded a servant when they got married and refused not only to go out to work but to work in the house. Further evidence of the respect for marriage is seen in the fact that a woman who achieves it demands and receives more respect from her neighbours than she did prior to marriage.

The case of a malaria inspector who had been a traveller in dry goods illustrates the extent to which the male fear of marriage can go. X is a black man. He claims that during a year which he spent travelling all over the island he had intercourse with a different woman every night. This was told with an air of apology rather than of boasting, and in island conditions it is quite probable. He is now about forty and is living with a town girl of about seventeen. He is not quite sure whether he will marry her or not. On being pressed he said he could not really afford it.

A wedding is not a cheap affair for the average couple. The peasant or worker insists on having a feast to which all his friends are invited. The food and drink cost a great deal. Cars must be provided to convey the chief guests from the house to the church and so on. Musicians must be paid. These are the reasons which are given when one asks someone why they cannot afford to get married. In the eyes of a black man or woman to be married without this paraphernalia would be no marriage at all.

Here then are two valid reasons for the continuance of concubinage. The fear of a woman changing her behaviour, and the actual cost of the wedding. As in most parts of Europe, the bride's father or mother provides the wedding feast. The female's fear of marriage is not as strong as the male's. It is a negative reaction rather than a positive one. But the feeling that a man may ill-treat her once he is her husband exists quite strongly.

The woman has her independence guaranteed by concubinage. She can leave the man at any time, and he feels the same. In practice this does not take place but it is clear that the feeling of freedom, which is absent in marriage, is a powerful force in keeping such unions together.

Upper and middle class opinion in the island is excited from time to time by the prevalence of concubinage. The experiment of mass marriages was begun quite recently. Fifteen or twenty couples who have lived in concubinage for years are persuaded to get married simultaneously. A charitable institution provides the bridal dress and shoes, and a communal feast is held. In one instance, shortly after the wedding a couple who had been in concubinage for years approached the sponsor of the scheme and asked for a divorce. They said they now found it was impossible to live together and, as they had been married by the sponsor, they now wished to be divorced by her.

There is no moral sanction against concubinage. Church congregations addressed by a priest on their sexual immorality will appear shamed, but it is a momentary feeling and their behaviour will continue as before. The attitude of the orthodox clergy of all denominations is that the people are immoral and need to have the error of their ways pointed out to them in order to mend them. In actual fact the black people have an entirely different conception of sexual morality from the coloured and white sections.(4)

To the average black man the fact that he lives contentedly with his woman without the benefit of Church or Law cannot conceivably be immoral. He may be an assiduous churchgoer and he sees nothing contradictory in the two types of behaviour. All churches refuse the sacrament to those who are known to be living in sin. Baptism, however, is not refused in the case of illegitimate children. The strength of the institution is seen again in the fact that the continuous preaching against concubinage by the churches has little or no effect, yet the people are extremely religious.

Another factor affecting concubinage is the desire to have children. The woman feels that she has not fulfilled her natural function if she has not had a child. To the man it is a test of his virility to make a woman pregnant. The Christianity in vogue is based more on the Old than the New Testament. The Old Testament has many injunctions to 'go forth and multiply' which support the attitude of the people.

Women at the pre-natal clinic had very strong views about having children. They thought anything else was unnatural. A very small percentage admitted to a knowledge of birth control, but they were not keen on using such methods to prevent conception. On one occasion an Englishwoman addressed a series of meetings in Port Antonio on the subject of birth control. She had large audiences from all sections of the community, but the repercussions were somewhat unexpected. At the usual medical inspection at the largest elementary school in the town the children refused to be inoculated against typhoid as their mothers had told them that if they were they would be unable to have children when they grew up!

Feeling in the home varies when a young girl becomes pregnant. Generally a temporary fuss is made but eventually the parents 'come round'. Resentment occurs most often in the cases where it is impossible for the girl to obtain help from the man who is responsible. The attitude is not a moral but an economic one. The parents dislike the added responsibility. The whole attitude of the black people towards concubinage is summed up by the black woman who on being upbraided for living like an animal said: 'I don't live like no animal. I have lived faithful with Ezra for thirteen years, and all my six children are from him one.' She was making the distinction between concubinage and promiscuity.

In the status system of the society marriage undoubtedly commands respect. Therefore conflict may be caused by the desire of a woman to achieve that respect and yet to maintain the freedom which concubinage bestows. The conflict is not open. Women questioned as to the desirability of marriage generally reply in the affirmative, but there is not an active discontent expressed of their status as common law wives. A Roman Catholic priest who has worked for years in several parishes in the island stated that without exception in all the cases he had come across (which must have been several hundred) the woman had desired marriage. Death-bed unions must be excepted. Cases do occur when a man on his death-bed may wish to marry his concubine with whom he has been living for many years. She is apt to refuse, arguing that if she was not 'good' enough for him during his lifetime she is not 'good' enough now. That it is the male who is desirous of Christian marriage when dying shows that the male also recognizes the prestige value of such a union.

It is difficult to determine how far religion affects the situation. I have said that people living together are in many cases assiduous churchgoers, and that there appears to them to be no contradiction between their marital habits and the law of the church. Yet the death of the male forces the contradiction into prominence. This suggests that in the face of the crisis of death the pressure from the upper strata of the society creates that which the normal events of life are incapable of doing – a recognition of a Christian moral sense. The importance of death is dealt with elsewhere. It is sufficient to say here that an inadequate funeral is regarded as a serious stigma on the deceased and his kin.

The conflict in the woman is again expressed in the incidence of bastardy cases in the law courts. The majority of such cases are brought by women who have been deserted by their menfolk soon after the birth of the child. Some, however, are concubines of some years' standing. In such cases the woman may have been only temporarily deserted. But the fact that she does not allow the customary interval to elapse, as happens with married couples, and appeals for a maintenance order is significant. If she can force the man to contribute to the support of the child she gains prestige in the eyes of her neighbours. Of course the economic motive in such actions must not be discounted. If the woman is not in work she will bring the action more quickly. In general both money and prestige operate together.

In the parish of Portland in 1934 there were 202 bastardy cases. The town jurisdiction accounted for 114 of these. In 1939 there were 117 such cases in Portland.

Another aspect of concubinage is seen in terms of colour. Respectable black people, who may be married themselves, would rather their daughter became the mistress or concubine of a white or fair coloured man than marry a black man. This illustrates both colour values and the social inheritance of slavery.

Legal divorce does not assume much importance amongst the black folk. As in Britain before the war, it is an expensive process. The number of divorces for the whole island in 1942 was 941. Of these 524 were black, and 283 (just over 25 per cent) coloured.(5) Portland accounted for 39 (4·3 per cent) of the total number of divorces, of which 27 were black, 10 coloured, and 1 white.

Limited promiscuity is indulged in by both sexes from puberty until they settle down with a particular mate. If children are born of such fleeting unions the man either settles down with the woman or, as happens frequently, leaves her, and she brings a bastardy action. The figures given for bastardy actions are not a fair index of the frequency of the break-up of such unions as very often the woman does not trouble to bring the action, for the man may have left the parish and cannot be found.

The period from puberty to settling down is one of experiment. Both partners will discuss freely the merits and faults of their former partners with their friends, and proceed to describe the defects and otherwise of their current choice. Elders do not object to this practice and to some extent they encourage it by providing sleeping accommodation. This period of experimentation may possibly be the reason why when concubinage proper is entered the couple do not tend to separate. The trying out of various partners tends to introduce stability when a more permanent union is formed. It is very exceptional to meet a young man who has not had sexual experience. Judging by the number of mothers between fourteen and twenty the same is true of women.

The sanction given by the greater part of the society in the island is very similar to that given in European countries to the man's period of 'sowing wild oats'. In the island, however, approval is extended to the girl. In fact it can be said that almost complete equality is reached between the sexes as regards youthful sexual experience. No slur attaches to the woman who has borne children; it is taken rather as an example of her useful fecundity.

In relation to both concubinage and to limited promiscuity the tremendous influence of the Bible must be taken into account. The Old Testament stories of concubines and handmaidens have become part of the lives of the people so that they have Biblical sanction for their behaviour which is in contradiction to the teaching of the churches. This may explain the black people's lack of a sense of contradiction between their sexual behaviour and Christian morality. The Bible through the breach with cultural tradition has become their rationale.

The heading of general promiscuity includes that type of behaviour in which both sexes have relations with a number of partners simultaneously, or for a brief period with a particular individual. Such cases are fairly numerous in the town but less so in the parish as a whole. The less settled conditions of employment in Port Antonio tend to a general restlessness which is exemplified in this sexual behaviour. Public opinion amongst the black people is inclined to be against too open a promiscuity, but there are no sanctions against it. Climate and facility as possible factors have also to be taken into consideration.

Polygamy generally arises in a definite economic setting. In the island as a whole its greatest frequency is found in the sugar parishes – the areas where the main occupation is working on the sugar estates. This is seasonal labour. The period of greatest employment is crop time which is from December to March. The result is that men and women tend to migrate in search of work in the off season.

Students of the University of the West Indies, Mona, Jamaica

The Campus of the University of the West Indies, Mona, Jamaica. *Photo:* Amador Packer, Kingston, Jamaica

A regular pattern is for a man to work on the estate in crop time and then to drift to the town in the off season in the hope of finding casual employment there. He tends to have a concubine and a complete household on or near the sugar estate, and in town he will have a similar establishment. Portland is not a sugar parish in the sense stated. The influence is seen, however, in the fact that some black workers in Port Antonio have places in the country a good distance away and have two establishments on the pattern of the sugar parishes. But the incidence of this is not very widespread.

The participants in all these types of behaviour may be and often are habitual churchgoers. There is no outward conflict exhibited. The attitude as has been said is openly amoral. Prestige may be lost by too open a promiscuity, but certainly not if the man or woman possesses a little money.

The brown and black middle class have a dual attitude towards concubinage and marriage. Behaviour is not affected by colour to any extent. Nor is economic position necessarily the determining factor. The two attitudes are: (*a*) a rigid conception of marriage, and (*b*) an indulgence in more or less open concubinage.

In (*a*) the norm is Christian marriage. The moral code is extremely strict. Any lapse is treated with severity and the individual concerned is ostracized. The behaviour of this section of the middle class is in marked contrast to the rest of the population. The emphasis is even greater amongst the black than amongst the coloured element. This is clearly due to the system of colour values. The black middle class person if he or she is to maintain the respectability which is the theoretical ideal of the middle and upper classes must maintain a rigid moral attitude as any deviation is treated as typical black behaviour by the upper classes. In other words there is a compulsion morality. This leads at times to neurotic outbreaks in the from of promiscuous behaviour. Such outbreaks are, however, comparatively rare. Given the general atmosphere of sexual opportunity the self-imposed restraint of this section of the middle class produces tensions which are seen in the rigidity of class patterns in other directions.

When an individual has a temporary lapse into promiscuity, the ostracism he experiences as a result is not permanent. He can overcome his mistake or breach of the ethical code in the passage of time, and can recover almost the same position as he held prior to the lapse. People in this section feel that they are the guardians of the morality of the island. It is suggested that their intense moral feeling is the result of frustration in other directions, for example their inability to rise socially because of their colour or lack of money. They appear to despise the behaviour of both the lower and upper classes.

In the section of the middle class denoted as (*b*) lip service is paid to the ideal of Christian marriage, but conformity is casual. The usual pattern is for a man to have a legal wife and children and a separate establishment for his concubine and her children. Or he may indulge in promiscuous activity with the knowledge of his wife and neighbours. This section of the middle class is somewhat fluid in its attitudes; a man will indulge in promiscuity for years and then will quietly settle down with a wife, and thus graduate to the more rigid section of his class. On the other hand he may remain in concubinage or promiscuous relations all his life with or without a wife as the case may be. This group in the middle class is despised by the other, but this has little effect in curbing its behaviour. There is little strain in this section as individuals appear not to care for the admonishings of their own class or the upper class. Individuals in section (*a*) however much they may object to the behaviour of individuals in section (*b*) will not admonish them openly. Here is an example of class solidarity due to the general uneasiness of the social position. The distinction between these sections is purely concerned with a Christian moral and religious outlook, there is no economic differentiation. They both unite in condemning black concubinage.

That general and limited promiscuity are found in section (*b*) is clear from the above. In section (*a*) general promiscuity is not tolerated. Limited promiscuity, however, does occur amongst youths. Parents do not attempt too violent a check as it is regarded as a necessary evil; 'the period of wild oats', etc. This is an example of an infraction of the moral code condoned in the face of apparent sexual necessity.

The Chinese constitute a separate section of the middle class. The invariable Chinese pattern is dual. Nearly always the man marries a Chinese wife. Concubinage is practised at the same time. Concubines are drawn from the black and coloured lower class. There is no racial antipathy on either side. In fact black women frequently express their liking for Chinese as their 'Sweet Man', or keeper.(6) This is due to the fact that the Chinese are famous for the care they lavish on their concubines as opposed to the casual treatment often exhibited by the coloured islander. The 1943 Census figures give the total Chinese population as 12,394. Of these 2,964 are married, and 601 have common law spouses. In Portland out of a Chinese population of 610,

134 are married, and 28 have common law spouses. These are not reliable figures as it is very probable that many Chinese returned as married have separate establishments for their concubines. The figures also include the number of Chinese coloured as well as pure Chinese, so no accurate statistical estimate can be derived from them. It might be suggested that religion is a bar to Chinese-coloured marriages, but out of 12,394 Chinese only 398 are listed as Confucians and Buddhists. In Portland there are 4 Buddhists and 7 Confucians. Thus the bulk of Chinese in the island are Christians, and so subject to a Christian ethic.

The Syrians who are divided between the middle and upper classes do not practise concubinage. The Census makes no mention of common law unions amongst them. The upper class Syrian tends to follow the normal upper class pattern. Middle class Syrians few in number tend to adopt the attitudes of section (*a*) of the black and coloured middle class. There are just over 1,000 Syrians in the island, of whom 50 are in Portland. The Syrians are either Roman Catholics or Anglicans.

The East Indian community is mainly concentrated in the sugar parishes and the urban area of the capital. Of a total of 26,507 7,036 are married, and 2,645 are living in concubinage. In Portland there are 1,484 East Indians, of whom 393 are married, and 173 living with concubines. In Jamaica as a whole 4,043 are listed as of the Hindu religion, and the rest are Christian. The same criticism is valid of these figures as of the Chinese. The pattern is intra-Indian marriage with the coloured woman as the mistress or concubine. The Indian community as such was not studied intensively.

All these alien groups are comparative newcomers in the settlement of the island. To some extent they have adopted the social modes and behaviour of the islanders, but not entirely. There is a definite conflict between the Eastern conception of family and woman as opposed to the islander's conception. Wives of the Syrian and Asiatic cannot be admitted to equality though the concubine is treated as an equal. The Eastern ethic is dying out as a force amongst the island born and bred Syrians and Asiatics.

The upper class is composed of fair coloured and white people. Their economic and social standing in the community allows them greater marital and sexual freedom than the middle class. The norm, however, is marriage. Though concubinage is not an accepted pattern cases do occur. There is a considerable amount of condoned adultery which in the capital takes the form of 'wife exchange'.(7) The amount of pre-nuptial sexual experience on the part of the younger generation is on the increase. Historically the upper class has always favoured concubinage, but in recent years there has been a reaction against it; the casual mistress has taken the place of the concubine. As the upper class is respected by all the other classes, their disregard for the marriage tie is accepted by them. The attitude of the middle class, section (*a*) is: 'While it is all right for them, it is not all right for us.'(8) The assurance which colour and economic position give this class enables it to have a far greater elasticity of morals and behaviour than is possible in the middle class. But it is an elasticity confined to the male.(9) The wife is expected and compelled to condone a mistress, but unless she is concerned in a wife exchange she is guarded against adultery. Both the upper and the middle class regard feminine infidelity as extremely heinous. A considerable degree of condemnation comes from the women themselves. This is another example of the so-called double standard of morals. The significant thing is that it is almost entirely absent in the lower class.

For the upper and middle classes divorce is an accepted institution. There are two contributory factors. The ability to afford the legal proceedings, and a moral code which admits divorce as a *solvent* of marriage. The figures given in Table 5 are significant as they show that there is a much higher proportion of divorce amongst whites (mainly upper class) than amongst any other section of the community.

TABLE 5

		Number of divorces	*Percentage according to number of marriages recorded*
Married whites	5,876	79	1·2
Married coloured	45,045	283	0·7
Married black	150,430	524	0·35

A wedding is regarded as an important event by all classes in the community. Three were witnessed by the writer.

A. LOWER CLASS WEDDING

On this occasion the parents of both the bride and the groom were peasants. The groom lived with his family in a town at the other end of the parish, and worked for a local fruit company. The groom and his parents were brown in colour. The bride was half East Indian, as her father was brown and had married a full blooded East Indian. He was a poor man and had about five acres of hillside land in the foothills of the Blue Mountains in Portland on the borders of the parish. The young couple had met at a dance in Port Antonio. Both the families were Anglicans. After a period of courtship lasting about a year, the banns were put up in the Anglican church in the town.

On the morning of the wedding the groom travelled from his home to meet the bride at the church. Only intimate guests attended the church, in which there were no special decorations. Everyone wore their best clothes; the women were in white or quiet colours with white shoes and stockings; the men were in their Sunday suits. The guests had come in cars hired by the bride's father for the occasion, though one car belonged to a guest.

The service was very simple and included an exhortation on the state the couple were about to enter. The whole procedure lasted about an hour including the interval of waiting for the bride to arrive. At the end of the service all the guests, with some additions who had arrived after the service, got into five cars and proceeded to the house of the bride's parents.

We were the last to arrive and although the cars were parked in the road we had difficulty in finding the house as it was not visible from the road. At last we found the approach by the bamboo 'draw-rail'. This consists of four or five rails of thick bamboo supported by two bamboo posts. It is of no real protection as it can easily be drawn, but it serves to indicate ownership. This 'draw-rail' was decorated with flowers formed into an arch. Behind it the hillside rose precipitously and we could see a path winding round and round the hill. The house, a two-roomed structure, was at the top of a very steep incline. The guests were not invited to go in, but were conducted to a specially constructed booth made of palm thatch and bamboo with an earth floor. The sole furniture was a wooden table and benches and chairs.

Before the meal began we were all served with very sweet wine in cups and glasses. A variety of toasts were drunk, but no speeches were made. The meal which followed consisted of curried goat, plantains, yams, cocoes, rice, and dasheens. The speechmaking began during the meal. Everybody was entitled to make a speech, and almost everybody did. Some of the peasants addressed the couple, who both looked very self-conscious throughout the speeches, as Mr and Mrs Bridegroom. The speeches were mainly about local events, the characters of all taking part in the wedding, and what the future held for the happy couple.

After the meal, which had begun about two o'clock and ended about four in the afternoon, people walked about the booth and drank neat rum. The peasants always drink rum neat. The wine was not served again. Wine is regarded as a great luxury and is only produced on special occasions. When the booth was cleared many of the men began games of dominoes which, as always, were played with great shouts and thumps on the table. Others looked on or walked about and chatted.

As dusk came on the musicians, who had long been expected, arrived. They were three men carrying a drum, a cornet, and a guitar. We all proceeded to the house in which the living-room had been cleared. It was quite a small room lit by an oil lantern which hung in the centre. Chairs were set for the musicians who first began to play island mentoes or borues. Couples began to dance, and then the bride's father called for a set, which is a dance derived from Sir Roger de Coverley. This was followed by a minuet, then an ordinary jazz tune of American origin. The changes were rung on these rhythms for the rest of the night. The bride and groom now appeared – she had changed from her wedding dress to her 'going away' clothes as they were to leave the same night for his home town. In fact they did not leave before midnight, and the party continued until early next morning. Some of the guests drifted away, but more were coming all the time as the night wore on. Rum was consumed continuously and the domino playing continued during the dancing.

The guests were not all peasants. Several dignitaries from the Parish Council had been invited, and had come. One fair coloured man had come from the capital. He had been the bride's father's commanding officer in the 1914 war. The father's land had been given to him after that war by the government.

The food and drink were lavish considering the economic position of the bride's father. I was told that the whole wedding must have cost about £30. This is a considerable outlay for a peasant. But there could have been no wedding unless it had followed the pattern described, as the parents would have been ashamed to have made a poorer show.

The former commanding officer was the fairest man present. Most of the other guests were black though there were quite a few brown people. All classes were represented, though it was noticeable that there were no East Indians present, none of the bride's mother's relatives were there.

In the middle of the proceedings the bride's mother began to cry, and several women had to comfort her. Another incident was a violent quarrel between two of the peasant guests, a man and a woman. She was his concubine and he had refused to go to their home a mile or so away to see if the children were all right. He was having a good time and did not see why he should leave. He eventually consented to go after several guests had remonstrated with him.

The whole atmosphere of this wedding was that while everyone realized that it was the celebration of a marriage which had brought them together, they were all bent on enjoying the occasion as something distinct from that purpose. There was no real disorder or drunkenness despite the great quantity of rum which had been consumed.

B. MIDDLE CLASS WEDDING

The father of the bride was black, and he held a responsible position in an important local firm. Her mother was fair. The town gossips said that no one could understand why she had married her husband because his colour was so different from her own. He was, however, a man who commanded respect in the community for his efficiency at work. The groom's father, an ex-civil servant, was brown; his mother was fair brown. The bride and bridegroom themselves were both brown.

They were all Anglican and the ceremony took place at the church in the town. The guests came from all over Port Antonio, and several came from the capital. As in the case of the lower class wedding only the more intimate friends were invited to the church. The ceremony was conducted by the same parson, and followed the same lines as the ceremony first described. The address was very little different. The church, however, was more decorated and looked quite festive. In both cases the organ was used for the entry and exit of the bride. There were numerous cars at this wedding.

There were at least sixty guests at the reception, which was held at the bride's parents' house. Several of the guests were not middle class, but lower class, such as an old nurse – a favoured employee of the bride's father. There was much speechmaking but the content verged on the fatuous, and only one attempt, that of the parson, approached a serious topic. Drinks were served all the time, ranging from rum to champagne.

The guests were all dressed in their good clothes. At the church the women did not wear white, but dressed in soft quiet colours. The general atmosphere was that of a normal party with nothing to mark the occasion as a unique one except the speeches.

Many of the guests had not seen each other for a long time and they used the occasion to renew acquaintanceship. Dancing began late in the afternoon and continued until about 2 a.m. The bridal couple had left for the capital for their honeymoon by ten o'clock. At the lower class wedding there had been no mention of a honeymoon, as the bridegroom had had to go back to work almost at once.

The colour range of the guests was quite wide but the class range, with the exceptions mentioned above, was small. Browns predominated, and there were very few blacks. No one quite as fair as the bride's mother was present.

Both these weddings indicate that an important aspect of such occasions is the opportunity to express class and colour solidarity.

C. UPPER CLASS WEDDING

This affair was in marked contrast to the other two. The church ceremony was the same except that the decorations were more lavish. Some of the guests felt slighted because they were not invited to the church. The bride's father was light brown, and he had 'good' features and 'bad' hair. His wife was very fair. The bride was fair, but her hair inclined to the 'bad'. The groom and his parents were all fair. The groom's father was a government engineer as was the groom himself.

Guests were invited from all over the island, and those from afar definitely outnumbered the local guests. The food was specially brought from the capital. Everything was done to mark it out from any local affair. Dancing followed the reception, which was held in the hall of the bride's father's office. Champagne was liberally dispensed. Soon after the speeches at the reception the couple left by car for the mountains for their honeymoon.

There were two exceptional incidents at the reception. One was when the groom's father refused to make a speech of congratulation because of his disapproval of the match (probably caused by the bride's father's colour). The other was when a local character, a black woman notorious for her sexual irregularities, attacked the character of the bride to the consternation of those guests who had not yet entered the building.

Although the custom is for the reception to be held in the house of the bride's parents, there was one instance, at a middle class wedding, when the house of friends was borrowed because the bride's house was too small. No adverse comment was passed on this by middle class people.

The common factor linking these different class weddings is the strength of class solidarity which they illustrate. Colour tends to follow class lines and vice versa. In the upper class wedding practically all the guests were fair, the exception being the local government officials who had to be invited because of their position. In the lower and middle class weddings blacks and browns, respectively, predominated. A lower class wedding is an opportunity for the black peasants to amuse themselves on what is for them a large scale. In all classes it enables individuals to exhibit that strong sense of 'family' or kin, which is characteristic of all islanders.

From the preceding analysis the factors underlying the pattern of behaviour obtaining in marriage, concubinage, and promiscuity can be distinguished.

Sexual impulses have been given expression in the concubinage-marriage pattern by certain social forces which are themselves the result of a peculiar historical process. Today the economic background of the society fosters the continuance of the pattern by maintaining the bulk of the population at an extremely low level of existence. Religion and morality as concepts in the Christian sense do not affect the behaviour of the lower class individual. He has created his own sexual morality which is rationalized by the Old Testament. He feels that he may be doing wrong only when he is brought face to face with the standards of the other classes in the person of the parson. This morality is so opposed to the usual Christian ethic that it has to be termed amorality, and it must be seen within its own terms. If the individual is a morally conscious being, which few are, he may appreciate the morality of the other classes as perhaps bringing more prestige if adopted, but not as being of value in itself.

The middle class is divided in the attitudes it adopts and in the behaviour which results. The duality does not follow colour lines, but it is symptomatic of the uneasiness caused by colour. The puritanical section of this class is scared of any behaviour which might reflect on their colour and class. The unpuritanical element accepts the inevitability of its position in society, and therefore does not attempt to curb its behaviour. The former section is as intent on the maintenance of its position in society as it is aware of its uncertainty.

It cannot be maintained that the pattern described is the result of conflict between African and European cultural traits. There is no evidence that African polygamous marriage and its attendant ethic persisted in the island.(10) On the other hand there is ample evidence that the European conception of marriage and concubinage acted as an example to the slave population. The real conflict is contained in the society itself – it is one which is evolved by the society. That is, the particular behaviour pattern is the manifestation of the degree of disequilibrium typical of this society. The insecurities of colour and of the economy are to some extent translated into moral and marital behaviour.

NOTES AND REFERENCES

1. *Registrar-General's Report*, Jamaica, 1942. In Port Antonio the records of the local Registrar of Births and Deaths show that in the period from October 1946 to the end of January 1947 there were 187 births, 119 of which were illegitimate – approximately 63 per cent.
2. Figures taken from *Census of Jamaica*, 1943.
3. Ibid.
4. See A. C. Kinsey, *et al.*, *Sexual Behaviour in the Human Male*, N.Y., 1948, pp. 384–6, for a discussion of different levels of sexual morality in a single community.
5. See Table 5.
6. Many black and coloured lower class folk believe that the male Chinese possesses remarkable sexual powers. It is similar to the belief among whites in the U.S.A. with relation to the Negro.
7. Two men will agree to exchange wives in order to clinch a business deal.
8. Condonation of concubinage by these classes does not extend to the lower class. The view is expressed that such behaviour on the part of black people is due to their inherent immorality and blackness.
9. Mistresses are drawn mainly from the lower class.
10. The contrary view is expressed by the late M. J. Herskovits in *The Myth of the Negro Past*, N.Y., 1941, pp. 143–206.

CHAPTER VI

The Lower Class Family – Family Structure

IN considering family structure in Jamaica it soon becomes clear that the contemporary form of that structure has arisen from a complex of factors. It is difficult to distinguish the exact influence of any particular factor or group of factors.

The writer contends that the forms which family structure has taken in the West Indies as a whole are *sui generis*. They are essentially a product of the peculiar conditions of slavery. To some extent these forms may have been influenced by the fact that the slaves were largely drawn from polygamous groups; but the dominant influence has undoubtedly been that of slavery itself.

A contrary view, that West African forms have survived into the contemporary scene, has been advanced by Herskovits.(1) Substantiation of this would depend for example upon demonstrating that patrilineal influence in Haiti has produced a different type of family organization from that which is extant in Jamaica, where the predominant influence appears to have been matrilineal. Herskovits's own field material on Haiti shows that this is not the case.(2)

Leyburn has shown that Haitian slaves were drawn from a number of different African groups.(3) Freyre has produced similar evidence for Brazil.(4) This would seem to suggest that as the slaves in the New World were drawn from a great area of Africa it would have been impossible for any one culture to survive as a whole. In other words the mixing of matrilineal and patrilineal groups in a particular area would have prevented the development of a society of one or the other specific type.

What in fact occurred was that these diverse groups were subjected to the uniformity of slavery. The manifestations of slavery in the New World were very similar; all were concerned with the exploitation of the Negro. The slave was able to perpetuate those aspects of his culture which were in essence secret such as magic, divination, and religion, and those aspects which were dependent upon a verbal tradition. The varied expression of such cultural traits, in the form of cult groups, illustrates the capacity of such verbal traditions to survive. But in the sphere which was controlled by the master, family life, the slave was forced into a new uniform mould. That mould was similar all over the New World in its major aspects. The pattern of European-African concubinage and the impermanence of slave sexual relationships is repeated from Brazil to the United States.

With the exception of the 'Bush Negro' of Dutch Guiana(5) who has through isolation evolved a matrilineal family pattern which owes little to slavery, the contemporary family structure amongst the New World Negroes can be distinguished as a phenomenon due mainly to the influence of slavery.

In a particular area, the Caribbean, the illegitimacy figures for the different territories fall roughly between 50 per cent and 70 per cent of the total of live births.(6) This indicates that the so-called deviation from the norm of Christian monogamous marriage appears to be fairly uniform over the whole area. It is suggested, therefore, that a single type of family organization exists throughout the Caribbean.

The primary family grouping is that of the elementary biological family, consisting of a man, a woman, and their children, real and socially ascribed. There has been a tendency to equate family with marriage, but as Linton points out: 'The personnel and function of this group [conjugal group] may coincide with those of the authentic family in certain societies, but they do not do so for human societies as a whole. Marriage and the family are really separate institutions and must be considered separately.'(7) The tendency towards this equation is due to the fact that in Western Europe this coincidence normally takes place so that dissociation appears difficult when dealing with other societies.

For the purpose of analysis it is necessary to divide Jamaican society into three classes; the lower class, 85 per cent of the population; the middle class, 10 per cent; the upper class, 5 per cent. The analysis which follows is concerned with the lower class, that is with the bulk of the population.

Family groupings can be divided into those with a conjugal and those with a consanguineous basis. That is into those which stress the husband-wife relationship, and those which emphasize the blood relationships of either the father or the mother. Western Europe exemplifies the former, and certain African areas the latter.

Jamaican family structure does not fall clearly into either category but appears to combine factors in both. There is, however, a tendency in certain types of family grouping to stress the husband-wife relationship. But there is not the same recognition of the monogamous conjugal union as the licit and morally approved means of satisfying sexual needs as there is in Western Europe. If this deviation is recognized the best method of classifying family groupings appears to be the adoption of the term domestic group as the unit of family structure in the island.

In Jamaica the domestic group is the residential unit which constitutes a household. The domestic group may, but does not always, consist of the elementary biological family; a man, a woman, and their real and socially ascribed children. It exists to satisfy the needs of sexual gratification, procreation, child-rearing, common housekeeping, and other domestic needs, protection of the group, and needs associated with social standing in the community. A domestic group may subserve all these needs, or only some of them, according to its actual constitution.

Four types of such groups can be distinguished:

A: Christian Family.
C: Maternal, or Grandmother Family.
B: Faithful Concubinage.
D: Keeper Family.(8)

This classification is not rigid as a domestic group can during its history experience several or all of these forms. Also there are groups which exhibit features of more than one type of group. But for analysis it is necessary to make a broad classification.

Marriage is the cohabitation of a man and a woman with the legal and social sanction of a particular society. Type A is the only form of domestic group which is based on marriage. The others have apparent community tolerance but no legal sanction. Jamaica is thus the example of a society in which there is a contradiction as regards conjugal unions between what is legally accepted as the norm for the whole society, and what is actually socially accepted. This contradiction or opposition between legal and social acceptance applies to other institutions as well as the family.

A domestic group, therefore, coincides with the legal family only in a minority of cases. These cases are confined to a section of the lower class, the middle class, and the upper class, which recognize Christian marriage as a legal and social norm. Common law marriages which are recognized for certain purposes at law, such as inheritance and maintenance, cover all those cases which are not described by Christian marriage. This distinction between Christian marriage and common law marriage is official and legal but is quite useless sociologically. Domestic group is a term covering all forms of familial relationships and in conjunction with the classification adopted is used in that sense.

Cohabitation is the mark of the domestic group of types A, B, and D, but it is not apparent in the case of C. A domestic group does not depend on the presence of cohabitation. Its presence helps to determine the type of family but not the existence of the family.

It must be emphasized that the classification of family groups is not of such fundamental importance as the functions of such groups in the society.

Stability and continuity in the family are more assured where there is a greater emphasis on the consanguineous as opposed to the husband-wife relationship. That stability is exhibited to some degree by the society considered.

The total number of mothers in Jamaica in 1943 was 258,842. Approximately 34 per cent were listed as married, 54 per cent as unmarried, and 12 per cent as widowed or divorced.

The attitude towards legal marriage is ambivalent. Unmarried mothers who are questioned will express a desire to be married, but frequently the same person will say that they are not sure of the man and wish to wait until they are, or until the right man comes along. Although no social stigma attaches to the unmarried state and 'living in sin' is not a term of reproach, marriage is often regarded as an ideal which is not within the woman's reach. Marriage to the lower class woman means a better home and above all a servant. Many Christian households were found in which there was a servant. In other words the economic factor is of some importance in determining legal marriage. The majority of cases of monogamy were found amongst the better-off members of the lower class. A typical case would be a man who combined peasant proprietorship with working as a carpenter or factory hand. As has been stated elsewhere another economic aspect is the actual cost of the wedding. The Jamaican insists on a 'show' at his wedding. People must be entertained with music, rum, and food; if this cannot be done it would not be a 'proper' wedding.

Another fear expressed by unmarried mothers is that marriage will lead to undue domination of the woman by the man. This may be a very real fear as there is no doubt that the monogamous union is a family strictly ruled by the husband-father, whereas in the unions B, C, and D, the woman is quite often the dominant member of the family. In practice the unmarried union leads to equality between the sexes.

The majority of the lower class is black as is the majority of the better-off section of this class. Colour operates in the usual way in governing the choice of a mate – an attempt is always made to secure a woman lighter in complexion and with 'better' features and hair.

The typical monogamous family will live in a three-roomed wooden house with a corrugated iron roof. One room is a living-room, the others are bedrooms. There may be more than one bed for the children. This is of great importance as it affects their early sexual habits. The fact that they do not sleep in the same room as their parents is of equal importance. There is usually a veranda where the family gathers in the evenings and where friends are entertained. The house will probably have electric light if it is in a town. In physical layout the home is a simplified version of the middle class home.

The father usually has a regular job and a small cultivation which may be adjacent to the house, or up in the 'bush'. He may be the sole wage earner unless the boys are old enough to be working, that is about fourteen years old. He will give his wife money for household expenses but there is no question of him turning over his weekly earnings to her. He is the final authority in all disputes in the home. The children attend school regularly and have more or less adequate clothing to wear. The whole family will be assiduous in its church-going. There is usually enough food but it may not always have a sufficiently high nutritive value. Such a household may consist of the man, his wife, and anything from two to eight children of the couple, the man's mother though rarely the wife's mother, the father's sister and her children, and the servant. The position of the servant and the institution of the 'schoolgirl' will be discussed in reference to the middle class family.

On all small matters and things concerning the daily running of the house the mother is the authority. She gives the servant orders and goes to market and so on. But anything requiring a more than routine decision is referred to the father. In disputes between the husband and the wife the father's mother often takes the side of the wife. Normally she does not interfere in the house. The wife does not attend to the cultivation unless she wishes to and the husband does not force her to do so. He works the cultivation much as the English allotment-holder does, in his spare time and at weekends. The wife may sell the produce in the market or get a friend to do so but she must account to the husband for the money.

Disputes are frequent in the family when the children reach adolescence. They may be caused by the choice of work for the boys or because the girls are running wild with boys. In some cases the children will leave home either to get a job in the capital or to live with some other family. The father will enforce his authority with a belt or a strap. Children are subjected to physical punishment from a very early age.

Meals tend to be taken in common and this acts as a binding force for the whole family.

The picture which emerges is reminiscent of the respectable Victorian working class family where the husband was a sober and steady person in regular employment. The atmosphere is markedly religious and the patriarchal attitude of the father is constantly reinforced by frequent reading of the Bible.

The maintenance of this type of domestic group is in part governed by the regularity of the man's employment so that there is an economic stability in the family. His sexual needs are satisfied within marriage. If he does feel the temptation to be unfaithful, religion and the concept of respectability are liable to prevent him. To do so would be to betray his group and to place him with the undesirable element of his class. The strength of this feeling is considerable.

Although a larger income is one of the factors which tend to produce monogamy it is only contributory, as there are many instances of better-off couples in the lower class who are not married. It is possible that the section of the lower class which comes in category A may have preserved some of the traditions of the groups of peasant people which after emancipation were filled with religious enthusiasm.(9) Such families are proud of their church connexion which may date back two generations or more. It is, however, impossible to say what are the precise motivations which cause one section of the lower class to adopt the manners and morals of the middle class as opposed to the majority of its own class.

The line of demarcation between types B Faithful Concubinage, C the Grandmother or Maternal Family, and D the 'Keeper' Family is not as clearly defined as it is between these forms and type A, the Monogamous Union. There is a tendency for types B, C, and D to coalesce together. A given family unit may experience all these forms during its lifetime.

Type B can be described as the type of family in which the man lives with the woman as if he were married to her and performs all the functions of a legal husband. In such a household there is a much greater sense of equality between the couple than there is in the Christian family. Many women say that they dislike the idea of marriage as it means being under the rule of the man. Such expressions are more common amongst the couples who have been together only a few years and tend to disappear as the household persists in time.

The Grandmother or Maternal Family is so called because the grandmother or some female relative, perhaps a sister, usurps the function of the father and at times that of the mother. Such a family can originate through the girl becoming pregnant while still living at home. The household may consist of her mother, her mother's sister, and the girl's siblings. The girl may remain at home and look after her child, but in many cases she leaves and the child is brought up by its grandmother. The girl's child is treated in the same way as the other children in the household, no distinctions are made. If the girl's father lives in the house he will act towards his grandchild as if it were his own child.

There are thus two types to be distinguished in category C. One where there is no male head of the family and the grandmother or other female relative fulfils the function of both father and mother; and the other where the grandmother may stand in the place of the mother but a man is nominally the head of the household.

Pressure may be brought to bear on the father of the child by the girl's family to make him contribute to the support of the girl and the child. She may even have him brought before the court and seek a bastardy order. But often neither remedy is effective as the man may have left the district and his whereabouts are unknown. Additional income may be brought into the family if the girl stays and works locally. In many instances she will move away and send money to her mother for the care of the child. When she has settled down with another man she will send for her child.

In the case of D the 'Keeper' Family the man and woman live together in a temporary union. He will contribute to her support but she may continue to work depending on how much money he brings home. If the union persists over a period of years it will come under the heading of Faithful Concubinage. The arrival of children may affect the continuance of the union. For the presence of several children often tends to drive the man away as it makes greater demands on his income.

It can be seen from the description of types B, C, and D that the psychological and domestic atmosphere of these households differs radically from that of the monogamous union. In C the child grows up with no knowledge of its father. The same can be said of D, as by the time the child is of an age to notice its parents the father may have left the house. Only in the case of Faithful Concubinage do these conditions approximate towards those of the monogamous union. The female partner in the 'Keeper' Family is constantly aware of the insecurity of her position which is the price she pays for her freedom from restrictions. It must be noted here that although the latter union is on a basis of equality, either partner is liable if the union is broken up against his or her will to resort to Obeah or violence. This is the case in all types of domestic groups, with the lowest incidence in category A.

It is difficult to make any accurate estimate of the incidence of the different types of families, as the Jamaica Census has no classification of class groups. A rough estimate from observations in the field would be that of all households, 25 per cent would come under the heading of Monogamous Union, 25 per cent under Faithful Concubinage, and the remainder divided in an inexact proportion between C and D.

C and D tend to occur more in the younger age groups in the period of sexual experimentation, but they are by no means confined to such age groups. The incidence for town and country does not seem to vary in any marked way.

The latter statement is of importance as it illustrates the fact that the Jamaican family structure is not due to the degeneration of a rural culture by corrupting urban or industrial influences, as was the case of the Southern Negroes migrating to the Northern cities in the U.S.A.,(10) but that it is a natural development of Jamaican society.

Actual living conditions are of vital importance, not in determining the type of family, but in affecting the norms of behaviour inside a particular type.

There are 16,528 dwellings in the parish of Portland of which 88·3 per cent are single storey cottages. Over half (57·9 per cent) of all dwellings are less than 150 square feet in floor area. These cottages usually have walls and floors of wood and a roof of corrugated iron. The kitchen is always a separate building often of a most primitive nature, generally a palm thatch shelter. Cooking arrangements are on the same level; an iron stove of Victorian pattern or merely a stone hearth is the most common. Sixty-three per cent of these cottages have no water supply. Water has to be fetched from a distance of anything from a few yards to a mile. Nearly 90 per cent of the people are without a bath or wash-house and the stream or stand pipe in the yard (garden) acts as a substitute. Of the total number of dwellings only 216 possess a water closet; 2,452 have no toilet facilities whatsoever, and the rest use pit latrines. It may be noted that there are frequent prosecutions for neglect either to build or maintain a latrine. These buildings are frequently infested by termites. Only 7·9 per cent of houses in the parish are classified in the 1943 Census as being in good condition and free from termites.

The great majority – approximately 63½ per cent – of the houses are owned by the occupants. Of the remainder approximately 18 per cent are free tenants, that is tenants at will; the rest pay rent which varies from under 6*s*. a month to 20*s*. a month, but the majority pays under 6*s*.

It can be assumed from these figures that the great majority of the working class lives in one or two roomed cottages with the minimum of facilities, and their families are brought up in conditions which represent a sharp deviation from the norm of middle and upper class homes. It must be noted here that the attitude of the latter classes towards the living condition of the working class is that it is largely their own fault for not making a sufficient effort. But fair coloured people tend to say that such conditions exist because the lower class is black, hence it is incapable of living in any other way.

Table 6 illustrates the classification of heads of households according to conjugal condition and sex. Those classified as single and common law according to the Census, are covered by the categories B, C, and D noted above. The majority of those cited as widows are covered by the same categories.

The apparent disparity between the figures for the island as a whole and those for Portland can be explained by the fact that the former figures are swollen by the population of the capital where women have a greater economic independence due to the greater facility for employment. This results in a larger proportion of them being listed as heads of households. The actual figures for Kingston are 19,887 male, and 14,902 female heads of households. The individual figures for each parish give approximately a third of the heads of households as female. If the single, common law, and widow categories are taken together to form the family types B, C, and D, it is seen that there are 7,214 male as opposed to 3,667 female heads of households not sanctioned by law. That is approximately half of these families are controlled by the mother or the mother substitute, whereas in the case of monogamous unions barely an eighth are controlled in this way.

TABLE 6

HEADS OF HOUSEHOLDS

	Male	*Female*
Parish of Portland		
Total	12,226	4,302
Married	4,987	571
Single	2,928	2,549
Common law	3,950	36
Widows	336	1,082
Divorced	17	62
Not specified	8	2
Jamaica		
Total	221,832	100,777
Married	95,265	11,479
Single	52,386	66,409
Common law	67,691	508
Widows	6,116	21,911
Divorced	332	431
Not specified	42	39

Table 7 gives the percentage of the population of Portland and of Jamaica over sixteen years of age according to conjugal condition.

TABLE 7

	Portland Male	*Jamaica Male*	*Portland Female*	*Jamaica Female*
	Per cent	*Per cent*	*Per cent*	*Per cent*
Single	49·0	50·9	43·1	49·3
Married	27·4	27·9	27·6	26·3
Common law	21·3	19·1	21·5	17·4
Widows	2·1	2·0	7·7	6·9
Divorced	0·1	0·1	0·1	0·1

The majority of those classified as single would fall into categories C and D. It is difficult to assess the actual bachelor and spinster population as although an individual may say that he or she is living alone, this may only be a temporary state prior to entering into a fresh arrangement with a partner of the opposite sex. It can be seen that the figures for the parish reflect those for the island. There is a slight variation from parish to parish but the consistency of the figures shows that the family-marital pattern detailed earlier is common to the whole island.

NOTES AND REFERENCES

1. M. J. Herskovits, *The Myth of the Negro Past*, N.Y., 1941, pp. 143–206.
2. M. J. Herskovits, *Life in a Haitian Valley*, N.Y., 1937, pp. 105–22.
3. J. G. Leyburn, *The Haitian People*, New Haven, 1941, p. 135.
4. Gilberto Freyre, *The Masters and the Slaves*, N.Y., 1946, pp. 298 et seq.
5. M. J. and F. S. Herskovits, *Rebel Destiny*, N.Y., 1934.
6. See Chapter V.
7. R. Linton, *The Study of Man*, N.Y., 1936, p. 173.
8. Professor T. S. Simey in his *Welfare and Planning in the West Indies*, Oxford, 1946, pp. 82–3, distinguishes four types of family groupings based on the researches of Mr Lewis Davidson: (*a*) the Christian Family, (*b*) Faithful Concubinage, (*c*) the Companionate Family, (*d*) the Disintegrate Family. The writer is indebted to Professor Simey for the nomenclature of his types A and B.
9. See J. M. Phillipo, *Jamaica : Its Past and Present State*, London, 1863, Chapter XVI, pp. 305–403.
10. E. Franklin Frazier, *The Negro Family in the United States*, Chicago, 1946, pp. 271–91.

CHAPTER VII

The Lower Class Family – Economics of the Family Structure

It has been estimated according to the 1943 Census that there are 194,458 people comprising the wage earning population of the island. The following tables show the correlation between colour and economic status, and between economic status and the proportion of women engaged in a wage earning capacity according to colour.(1)

TABLE 8

ISLAND WAGE EARNING POPULATION

Colour	*Total*	*Male*	*Female*
Total wage earning population	194,458	123,890	70,568
Black	151,101	96,878	54,223
Coloured	33,640	19,976	13,654

TABLE 9

	Wages under 6s. a week	*Wages 6s. to 10s. a week*	*Wages 10s. to £1 a week*	*Wages £4 to £5 a week*
Black	48,155	40,022	40,226	554
Male	18,285	25,773	32,621	512
Female	29,870	14,249	7,605	42
Coloured	5,502	5,299	7,317	1,083
Male	1,941	2,741	4,163	838
Female	3,561	2,558	3,154	215
White	36	32	510	289
Male	14	24	291	167
Female	22	8	219	122

It is clear from these tables that the black people supply the largest group of workers at the lowest income level, that is under 6*s*. a week. They are also the only group in which the women workers outnumber the men. As income increases amongst the black group the number of women employed drops. This is not true for the other groups. The coloured group in the lowest wage classification exhibits the same phenomenon as the similar black section in that female workers outnumber the male. But a higher proportion of women are employed in the coloured section 10*s*. to 20*s*. group than in the black section. As regards the white section the first three income groups would be classified as poor whites – those who come from isolated white communities living at a low economic level. The Census does not list the planter and business groups which form the largest section of whites. It is interesting to see that in the under 6*s*. a week division the whites exhibit the same tendency as the other groups – to have more female than male workers. This is due to the high proportion of women of all colours in the lowest income group who are the sole supporters of families in the absence of the man, and to the fact that in B and D domestic groups, which are usually found at a low economic level, the woman tends to work as well as the man.

The economic structure of a domestic group varies according to its type. Further variation may occur dependent upon the behaviour of individual members of a particular household.

In the Christian Family with its patriarchal spirit the husband-father controls the greater part of the expenditure. He is the main economic support of the group. His wife may work and if she does her income goes into the general fund. The children who are employed are expected to make a definite contribution towards their keep. If a son-in-law becomes a member of the household he will contribute to its support. As will be seen its pattern is similar to that of the middle class family.

Superficially Faithful Concubinage appears to differ little from the Christian Family. There is, however, a difference in the function of the female partner. In this type of household a tendency can be discerned for the woman to have a greater share in economic activity, and even to dominate the economic relationship of the conjugal partners.

In the case of the maternal family the eldest female relative may exercise economic control over the rest of the family. Children at work are expected to contribute to the household expenses, and they generally do so, but compulsion may have to be exerted to this end. The whole economic structure is more flexible than in domestic groups A and B. The Keeper Family is really a partnership between the man and the woman. Generally an arrangement exists whereby they both keep their own earnings. The expenses concerned with the children will be borne by the mother. The feeling that the unit may break up at any time creates a situation in which exact economic differentiation is relatively unimportant. Contributions from children do not apply as by the time they are of employable age the status of the family will probably have changed.

It is hoped that this description has covered typical behaviour in the four types of domestic groups, but a great number of individual variations do occur. There are families in which the father does all the marketing himself, as he refuses to trust his wife or concubine with a penny. Other fathers living in Faithful Concubinage drink the greater part of their earnings, and their concubines have to do the best they can for themselves. There are even comparatively well-to-do peasants in any type of household who give their partners not only housekeeping expenses, but an allowance for themselves. But such behaviour is a deviation from the pattern – the majority of individuals appears to fall within the general description given.

The basis of the family income is the cultivation or small-holding, which is either owned by the family or rented. This may vary in size from a 'square' (a fraction of an acre) to ten acres or more. It supplies the family with a variety of food crops from the yam to the banana. The banana is the best cash crop. A guaranteed price dating from the war is paid by the government to the grower. Government also buys other crops such as yams, but the prices for the banana are the highest. What the family does not consume is sold either to the government or in the local market. Money must be obtained to pay not only the rent and taxes, but to purchase clothes, rum, tobacco, medicines, such articles of food as fats (generally coconut oil), and rice which is rarely grown except by East Indians. Obeah (witchcraft) is a major item of expense for many families. It should be noted that the soil of Portland is extremely fertile as compared with a drought-ridden parish such as St Elizabeth.

Below is a table of three lower class weekly household budgets. A is that of a Christian Family of four in fairly good circumstances. B is a family of three in the category of Faithful Concubinage. C that of a couple in a Keeper Family. The presence of vegetables as an item of expense is due to the fact that the cultivations in question are very small. In a typical peasant proprietor's budget these items would be absent. The cases are typical of many in Port Antonio.

There are several points to be noticed about these budgets. It appears that the expenditure for soap is about the same for all families as it is for starch. The Jamaican is a cleanly person both in his clothes and his body. He will go without something else rather

TABLE 10

Item	*Case* A	*Case* B	*Case* C	*Remarks*
	£ *s.* *d.*	£ *s.* *d.*	£ *s.* *d.*	
Electricity	5 0	—	—	
Yam	1 0	2 0	1 6	
Rice	10½	10½	10½	1 lb.
Flour	4½	9	4½	
Sugar	6	5	4	3*d.* a lb.
Meat	5	1 1½	9	5*d.* a lb.
Bread	2 0	2 0	1 0	2 lb. loaf 6*d.*
Milk (cow's)	2 4	1 6	9	9*d.* a qt.
Milk (tinned)	9	—	—	
Fish (fresh)	2 0	9	1 0	About 1*s.* a lb.
Fish (salt)	11	5½	—	
Butter	6	3	3	1*s.* a lb.
Cream (face)	2 6	—	—	
Vegetables	9	6	3	
Fruit	6	3	3	
Cooking oil	11	6	3	
Cocoa	6½	3	3	
Oats	10½	10½	—	
Salt	3	3	3	
Matches	1	1	1	
Fuel (cooking)	1 0	1 0	6	
Soap (toilet)	6	6	6	
Soap (washing)	5½	6	7½	
Starch	3	3	3	
Oil (light)	—	4	4	
Polish	6	6	3½	
Hair oil	—	3	9	
Thread	—	10½	—	
Writing paper	9	—	1 0	
Stamps	1 0	—	4½	
Children	8 0	—	—	
Total	1 15 11	17 4½	11 11½	

than sacrifice his cleanliness. Case A has no item for lighting oil as the house has electric light. The price of some of the articles is remarkable for a country which produces them. Sugar is 3*d.* a pound. The high price of bread is due to the fact that all the flour is imported from Canada. Butter is locally produced in limited quantities, hence its price. Canned goods do not appear in the budgets except for milk, which is canned locally. This is explained by the prohibitive price of such goods. It is clear that Case B spends very little on the children as there was no separate item for them.

As well as cooking for the household the woman is expected to look after everyone's clothes, mend them, and care for the home. These functions are most stressed in the Christian Family and least stressed in the Keeper Family. Domesticity can in fact be equated with stability. When the family has a stable basis both the man and the woman are able to have advantages which are lacking in a less stable situation. Stability is not a question of the duration of the group alone, but also of income fluctuations.

When the man is living in the group the woman relies on him to protect the family against any dangers. When he is not the protective duty devolves on the mother or mother-substitute, that is the eldest female relative; or alternatively on some adult male resident in the group.

The domestic group may quarrel within itself but it faces the world as a unit. If there is dislocation within the group this resolves itself in the face of a danger which threatens the entire group. When there are parent-children disputes which coincide with the threat of dispossession from the house, the parents and children will unite to fight the landlord. This solidarity is a marked characteristic of the domestic group.

NOTE

1. Based on those contained in the 1943 *Census of Jamaica*.

CHAPTER VIII

The Lower Class Family – Birth

IN the discussion of beliefs and practices which follows it is impossible to make a real distinction between rural and urban families. There is in fact no exact line of demarcation between the town and country. Surrounded as it is by land settlements, Port Antonio is really part of the country. It might be felt that the relative isolation of some rural districts would tend to foster superstition, but the prevalence of Obeah (witchcraft) practices in the town is as great as it is in rural areas.

Pregnant mothers can be divided into two categories: those who attend the pre-natal clinics (of which there are four in the parish) and who have their baby at the hospital in the town or at home with the district nurse in attendance; and those who call in the aid of the nana. The nana is an untrained midwife. She is generally an old woman without children living with her. She acts as the unqualified nurse for a district and is the source of all advice on mothercraft. These women have had no training in nursing or medicine but they are regarded as great sources of wisdom. They may or may not be Obeahwomen.

The first category of expectant mothers is in a minority. The choice of the nana in preference to the nurse is often due to the fact that the nurse will only give medical attention to the mother, whereas the nana will also look after the children and prepare the family's meal. The nana is of greater use to the mother than the nurse. She performs an extremely important social function – as a wise elder of the society she inducts the newborn child into the society. Another reason for the choice of the nana is the actual topography of the area. The parish of Portland is extremely mountainous as is the island as a whole. Most of the clinics are situated in coast towns. Often it requires a tremendous effort on the part of the pregnant mother to make the journey to the nearest town. Many of the settlements can only be reached by narrow mountain paths. In one case a young man who wished to obtain medicine from the doctor at the hospital for his concubine, who was pregnant, had to cross two rivers on foot and descend and climb mountains to get to the nearest town six miles away. When he returned with the medicine after several hours the woman was dead.

There may be cases of women who appear to fall into both categories; a mother who attends the clinic may also employ a nana. For example it is quite common at the town clinic to discover women who have a cord tightly tied round their waist. They will say that this is done on the advice of the nana to prevent the child in the womb from leaping up inside and suffocating the mother.

Folk beliefs persist together with modern medical practice. The writer witnessed several one-day clinics held in mountain villages by a Medical Officer of Health. It appeared as though the whole female population of the village and a great part of the male population had turned up at the clinic. One reason may have been the desire to test the efficacy of the doctor against local wisdom. But many women continue the home or folk treatment of ailments or pregnancy together with medical treatment.

When a lower class woman becomes pregnant she begins to take certain precautions. She must not step over a rope or a wire fence but must always lift it up. This seems to be an elementary precaution against jerking or twisting the body in case it may affect the child. The mother must not eat rich foods nor drink too much milk lest the child be born fat. If two or more pregnant women meet each must turn back and walk until she reaches a cross-roads so that she may take another path, thus they avoid passing each other. If the mother works hard the baby will be energetic. 'White people just stay in home and read book.' This refers to the fact that upper class pregnant women do not appear very often outside their homes. This also appears to be the custom in the United States unlike that prevailing in England.

At the time when the child is about to be born the nana takes charge. Her face is washed with rum, and she drinks some. This is to give her 'eyesight'. A nana will say that every time she witnesses a birth her sight is affected. If the labour is difficult the father is called into the room and a vest or shirt belonging to him is used to bandage the mother's waist. It must be a dirty shirt with his dried sweat on it; the mother smells the arms of the shirt; 'This helps the labour.' Or the mother may be taken to the father's favourite resting place which is sometimes outside the house.

When the baby is born it is slapped if it does not cry; 'If it don cry it going to be dumb.' If it is born with a caul it will be able to see ghosts. This is a very strong belief amongst the people. The afterbirth is taken and buried with a silver coin in the yard. The afterbirth must point in a particular direction otherwise: 'She won't have any more pickney [children].' If the navel cord has knots in it the nana counts them to see how many children the mother will have. When the remains of the cord fall from the baby they are planted beside a tree, which is usually a coconut palm. If the parents can afford it a special tree is planted. Dr Beckwith found that this tree must be cared for during the whole lifetime of the person concerned.(1) People nowadays do not seem to lay the same emphasis on the tree.

If the afterbirth will not come away quickly the nana gives an empty pint bottle to the mother who blows into it, but nothing else is done to expedite its passage. Sometimes during the actual labour the nana will anoint the mother's stomach with castor oil and put a cord round the waist. This is to help 'push down' the baby.

The birth of twins is not regarded as a special event. There is a certain amount of fear at the time of delivery but that is all. This fear is purely concerned with the suffering of the mother and the chances of both children surviving.(2)

If two pregnant women are living in the same house they will both carry about a sprig of a green bush in their hands or bosoms. No informant appeared to know the reason for this custom, nor the fact that many pregnant women will wear an iron nail in their hair.

It was stated earlier that the nana was an old woman past child-bearing age. Although most of them have had no specific medical training a few may have worked in a hospital as a ward maid, or as a servant in a doctor's house, and in this way have picked up some trifles of medical knowledge. They turn to their particular profession if they have no other means of support and have sufficient personality to impress people with their superior wisdom. It only requires one or two successful births for the nana to be established professionally. There may be several working in the same village.

In one case a nana was found blowing smoke into the newborn child's face: 'For the spirits.' But the connexion between the nana and Obeah is difficult to establish. At childbirth she is not paid for working Obeah, that is done quite separately. Yet the possibility of the two functions being combined in the same person cannot be overlooked.

The nana comes to the house on the day of the birth and for nine days afterwards. She does not sleep in the house. The average charge for her services is about 12*s*. In hospital the charge is 30*s*. for the same period.

In the town there are three certified midwives, and one Public Health nurse who acts as a supervisor. These midwives will attend births in the home but they will do no washing, cleaning, or cooking, etc. Their average fee is 21*s*. If the woman cannot afford it the hospital makes no charge. But people are slow to take advantage of this. However poor the individual may be, she does not like to admit it publicly. Some people prefer to pay the nana 12*s*. if they cannot afford the 30*s*. for the hospital. Or they would pay the nurse's fee rather than accept free treatment at the hospital and so make a public admission of their poverty. The midwives will accept less than their guinea but this again is admitting poverty. It may appear strange that in such a poverty stricken country it is regarded as a disgrace to be poor. Yet, as has been seen, the desire to conceal the existence of poverty is very active.

Although the influence of the nana is still very strong, there is a tendency for mothers to take advantage of nurses and the hospital when they are available without too much difficulty. This explains why the nana is still predominant in country districts and in the environs of the town, but in the central parts of the town 70 per cent of births take place in the hospital or at home with a certified midwife in attendance. The remainder of births is attended by a nana. In a sea coast village on the border between Portland and St Thomas (the adjacent south-eastern parish) all births were attended by a nana before the establishment in 1945 of a pre-natal clinic held once a fortnight.

The newborn baby is kept in one room for a period of from seven to nine days otherwise it will be dumb when it grows up. Visitors generally go to see the child after this period, and when they do, they take a gift of money. When the baby is first shown to people it is rubbed with washing blue and marked so that the ghosts will not play with it and kill it. A 'coolie red' – a polka dot cloth – is also wrapped round the child for similar reasons. The cloth is kept on for about three months. Up to three years a little black bag of asafoetida is kept tied round the child's neck on a piece of string. These bags are frequently found on children who are brought to the post-natal clinic in Port Antonio. Both this and the custom of kneading asafoetida into the membrane of the child's head before it closes are used as a protection against ghosts.

The baby must never be passed through the window or it will grow up a thief. If it is passed through it must immediately be passed back. People must not call the child pretty if it is pretty but say that it is ugly; and so on for all attributes. If this is not done the baby will die. When the child is bathed it must first be tossed in the air and caught by the feet and hands. A bowl of water and 'soap bush' (a green plant which when boiled makes a soapy mixture which can be used as soap) with two sticks crossed over the top is placed outside in the sun. Whenever the child is bathed it is given some of this mixture to drink.

To facilitate walking some mothers anoint the child with neat's foot oil. When the child begins to creep about and look under the mother's clothes it is said that it is looking for another one, that is the mother is pregnant again.

The belief in ghosts or duppies is very strong. If a small boy has long hair the parents give him money when they cut his hair. This is because every child has a good ghost and a bad ghost, and cutting the hair may annoy the good ghost so the money is paid to him. Adults have these ghosts as well. The good one is always taking care of the bad one. 'Sometimes you go to de bush [country parts] and you hear a stick break. It's de ghosts. And Bad One say to Good One, "Come, we kill him", the Good One says "No." Bad One, "Why not?" Good One, "Because he me cousin." Bad One, "How do you know?" Good One, "Just wait and see." The Good One takes up the stick and breaks it, you look round. Good One, "Same ting I tell you." [I told you so.]'

Children are brought up in this atmosphere of ghosts and spirits. Early in life they are frightened by being threatened with the 'Bugaboo' man and from then on there is always some explanation of a supernatural kind for everything unusual which occurs. An important fact bearing on this is that so many children are brought up in the ideas of two generations ago, that is by their grandmothers. The stories told to children are taken from the cycle of Anansi the Spider and his son Tacooma. They are concerned with the wiliness of the spider as compared with the strength of other animals. These stories are very similar to the American Uncle Remus cycle of Brer Rabbit. According to Rattray Anansi exists in Ashanti and his son is known as Ntikuma.(3) While the older generation is familiar with Anansi stories, they appear to be dying out in the present generation of young people.

The idea of a good ghost and a bad ghost, and the Anansi stories is the perfect illustration of the syncretism of Jamaican culture. The first may have been taken from European folklore of the seventeenth century indentured servants, while the other is obviously of African origin.

To the lower class Jamaican the world is full of mysterious events which can only be explained by reference to ghosts. Evil is produced by Obeah and can only be counteracted by more Obeah. The spirit world must not be ignored. Attention must be paid to it by doing the right things. This concept of the world may spring from lack of what is called education, or on the other hand from the isolated conditions under which many of the people live.

Christening is a universal practice carried out equally by church-goers and by those who have no particular religious belief. Sometimes an open Bible is found beside an unchristened child, or a cross marked over his bed in chalk. Both these practices are to keep away evil spirits. Unless the child has a name the spirits will have power over it.

The choice of a name for the child allows the Jamaican imagination full play. Many adult illiterates are familiar with parts of the Bible through hearing them repeated over and over again. In many homes the only reading matter is the Bible. Others buy or borrow the daily newspaper. Through this and the medium of the cinema most of the lower class are familiar with the names of film stars. These are the main sources of names for children. The most obscure names in the Old Testament are also met with in the island. A popular film star or a member of the royal family, the leading politicians in the island, world famous war leaders, all have their quota. This is a modern manifestation, as the older generation was content with the Bible for naming their children. One of the most frequent names for a girl was Icilda (a face cream). 'Wray and Nephew', the trade name of a famous spirit firm, was given to one child. Children are also named after boats and houses. The more religious section of the people is inclined to perpetuate the names of religious leaders and ministers.(4)

When the father is absent the child will take the surname of the mother, who continues to call herself Miss with no sense of impropriety. Professor Simey mentions announcements and photographs

Above : Pocomania Meeting House. *Below :* Peasant hut in Portland

The other Jamaica: upper class housing in Jamaica today. *Photo*: Quito Bryan

which appeared during the war in the daily paper which read: 'Private X, son of Miss Y, now serving overseas.'(5)

It is felt to be impossible for a person not to have a name even if it is what is called 'not a real name'. Children are given names of powerful people who it is felt will protect them. There is obviously a feeling that the attribute of power or influence associated with a great name will be transferred to another bearer of the name.

All religious groups insist on godparents at christening. Boys are supposed to have two godmothers and one godfather, girls vice versa. This is always supposed to have been so but no one can offer an explanation. The godparents are intended to be mutually responsible for the child but this rarely occurs. Most children do not know the names of their godparents. Some godparents are, however, active in their duties and give presents to the children from time to time. Sometimes a child is adopted by a godparent.

The function of naming or christening in the society appears to be the giving of identity not only with the group, but with the individual after whom the child is named. As has been seen it gives protection against spirits and generally serves to give solidarity to the community.

No attempt is made by mothers to prevent jealousy between the existing children and the new arrival. The result is that often the other children feel active resentment against the baby which may be translated into action against the infant. This in conjunction with other factors helps to create the general atmosphere of frustration which is so prevalent in Jamaican childhood. There tends to be a favourite amongst the children in most families. The father may prefer the first or only girl; the mother the youngest child. Or both may unite in showing favour to the fairest member of the family; 'She carry off the rest of us.' Thus colour frustration occurs from an early age.

The duration of breast feeding depends on whether the mother goes to the post-natal clinic or not. If she does she is given definite instructions to wean the child at eight or nine months. Mothers who rely on the nana may persist in breast feeding the child for eighteen months or longer in the belief that it prevents pregnancy. James West mentions a case in the American Middle West of a boy of five or six who was still unweaned.(6) Weaning is not gently induced; the breast is abruptly taken away and the baby is given a bottle of sugar water or corn meal pap instead. It is suggested that the prolongation of breast feeding in the society may help to explain the profound psychological dependence of the adult Jamaican on his mother. This gives a psychological background to the social situation in which the boy has often been deprived of a father's care and so has grown to place complete reliance on his mother.(7)

The induction of sphincter control is also a rough and ready process. The child is expected to control itself by the time it is a year old. If it messes unduly after that time it is beaten. As a result the frequency of eneuris and constipation is quite high.

NOTES AND REFERENCES

1. Martha Beckwith, *Black Roadways*, Chapel Hill, 1929, p. 55.
2. The attitude towards twins is quite different in Haiti. See for example M. J. Herskovits, *Life in a Haitian Valley*, N.Y., 1937, pp. 202–3.
3. R. S. Rattray, *Akan-Ashanti Folk Tales*, Oxford, 1930, p. 73.
4. An examination of names at many London Labour Exchanges will reveal similar peculiarities.
5. T. S. Simey, *Welfare and Planning in the West Indies*, Oxford, 1946, footnote, p. 88.
6. James West, Plainville, U.S.A., in Abram Kardiner, *The Psychological Frontiers of Society*, N.Y., 1945, p. 318.
7. This maternal reliance extends to the adult immigrant in Britain who before taking an important decision may well consult his mother back in Jamaica.

CHAPTER IX

The Lower Class Family – Growth and Youth

As the child begins to grow up it starts to help in the household. It has definite tasks allotted to it such as fetching water from the stream, helping with the cleaning of the cottage, and so on. Generally the child has no toys except what it may find or make for itself. Often children are kept locked up all day in the cottage while the mother goes out to work. Sometimes food is left within reach, but frequently they have to wait until she returns home before they eat. One family was seen on a land settlement near Port Antonio which was in charge of a girl of ten. She was cleaning the house while her brother cooked some fish over an open fire for the midday meal for the six children. The father and mother were both absent working.

The socializing process for the child is a contradictory one. On the one hand he may have impressed on him the necessity of not lying and of being kind. On the other hand he may be complimented for some little piece of sharp practice directed against 'them', that is people in a superior social position. Both parents but especially the mother will vary from extreme brutality in beating the child to excessive kindness. The child who has been subjected to such treatment tends to possess the same ambivalence of attitude when he is an adult. This is shown by his gentleness as a person in spite of the fact that the courts are so full of crimes of violence and cruelty.

The father generally plays a minor role in the life of the children. In many cases he is entirely absent from the household. When he is present he is not very much concerned with them, though one does occasionally meet a proud father. The children are the concern of the mother, and she in turn relies on *her* mother for information and instruction. In one case cited by a social worker the father did not even know the names of his twelve children.

Obedience is exacted by swearing at and often beating the child. Extreme cases have occurred of parents tying a child over an ant-hill, holdings its hands over a fire, etc. Making a child feel ashamed is also a deterrent but as this is done publicly it tends to produce inhibitions.

At the age of six or seven a child may begin to go to school. The elementary school population (children from seven to fourteen) for the whole of Jamaica is 234,519, out of which 80·6 per cent of the children attend school, and 19·4 per cent do not. For Portland the total population of school children between seven and fourteen is 11,466, of which 85·7 per cent attend school, and 14·3 per cent do not. These figures compare very favourably with the figures for the other parishes. For example in St Elizabeth, a larger parish whose total population is 100,182 as compared with Portland's total population of 60,712, the elementary school population is 21,003, out of which 72·9 per cent attend school, and 27·1 per cent do not. The general illiteracy rates for the two parishes are: Portland 20 per cent, St Elizabeth 34·6 per cent.(1)

The figures for school attendance are apt to be misleading. In a normal school week the attendance will decline progressively from Monday to Friday. One of the chief reasons for this is the lack of proper clothing for the child. Just as the Jamaican refuses to get married unless he can make a 'show', so he refuses to send his child to school unless it is properly clad. With poor families, which are the majority in this class, clothing is scarce. The child will have clean clothes on Monday, but if they are dirty on Tuesday they will have to be washed and the child will stay at home until Wednesday, and so on. Repairing clothes produces similar results. On a Thursday or Friday the child may have to go marketing, so he is absent from school. There are school attendance officers, but they are too few and their task is rendered difficult by the topography of the country.

Another factor affecting school attendance may be that an older child is often required to stay at home and look after the younger children while the parents are at work. The child may also be required to work in the field with the parents.

The great majority of parents regard education as a desirable thing. There are only a few illiterate parents who think education is a waste of time because they can see no difference between themselves and their literate neighbours. There are thus few who would prevent their children from going to school unless there was a very real reason like those stated above. Education is regarded as a means whereby a person may be lifted up from poverty and agriculture to become a clerk or a professional man. As those who do achieve these positions are few in number this attitude gives to the whole of education an unreal atmosphere. Vocational education is not considered as education in the proper sense. The tendency to associate manual labour with degradation, and to regard education as a means of eliminating manual labour is typical not only of Jamaica, but of many European countries with a peasant population.

Many children, though mainly those of Christian Families, are encouraged to work hard. If a child wins a scholarship to a secondary school the parents will strive to obtain a sponsor from the upper class who will assist the child financially. Or they may endeavour to keep the home going without the expected help from the earnings of the child after it leaves the elementary school.

Obeah too plays its part in the furthering of the child's education. Some people consult an Obeahman before making a decision about the child's future. The father may ask the Obeahman whether he should apprentice the boy as a carpenter or take him to work on his cultivation. But Obeah or the fear of it may act as a deterrent to encouraging the child to progress too far socially, as parents may think that jealous neighbours will get an Obeahman to 'fix' them if they allow their children to have advantages which the neighbours cannot afford for their children.

In school the socializing process of the child increases. He begins to meet and play with children from other homes. Teachers attempt to instil the virtues of truthfulness, honour, and gentleness. But it is a losing fight against the home environment. The child returns every afternoon to the meanness of perhaps one room, and is unable to put what he has learned into practice. The average lower class youth is taught at home to regard anyone in a superior social position as fair game for deceit. Teachers complain that it is very difficult to make their charges realize the error of lying and the virtue of truthfulness.

The dichotomy between home and school life is further emphasized in this way. Until a few years ago the textbooks used in the schools were illustrated by facts and objects which would be familiar to the European child but not to the young Jamaican. It is still claimed with some validity that the average Jamaican child knows more of the history and geography of Britain than he does of his own island.

At home the attitude of the parents towards sex instruction and masturbation varies. Most mothers tend to avoid giving sex instruction, perhaps because they realize that it has already been gained through observation in the home. But there is definitely a reticence to discuss sexual matters with children. If, however, instruction is given, it is almost always the mother who gives it. Masturbation is sometimes regarded as an evil but the mother may be too preoccupied to notice its occurrence. Some parents think that it will impair the virility of the child later on, and will attempt to curb it. Its prevalence may be due to the lack of toys and playthings for the child. This preoccupation with his own body does not seem to leave any discoverable mark on the adult.

As regards girls the same attitude exists on the part of the mother. Very few give any sensible account to the child at her first menses. Some even treat the girl as if she had committed some offence. One ignorant mother told her child: 'Yes, mi missus, the time yu don't see it you will tell me whey [where] it gone.'

The antithesis of these attitudes may occur where parents will deliberately encourage their children in their premature sexual activities, even with each other. But such cases are not common.

Up to about seven or eight years old there seems to be little difference in the parents' attitude towards boys and girls. At this age, however, a sex distinction is noted in that the girl is told not to run about in the same fashion as the boy. She is expected to take a greater interest in womanly things and so on. Modesty, up to about eight years of age, is often determined by lack of clothes. Very often children of both sexes will be seen runing about naked to this age. After that some effort is made to see that at least the girl is always clad, even if it is only in one garment. Children of different families bathe together nude up to ten or eleven and indulge in mild sex play when doing so.

Games played by boys are varied and follow a seasonal pattern as in England. Cricket is perhaps the most popular. It is played with a dried branch of the coconut tree as a bat. Football is also played, and marbles, flying kites and spinning tops all have their season. Girls play ring games and skip. None of the games appear to have a specific Jamaican flavour, but are all derived from Britain.

From the account given above it may be seen that no attempt is made either at home or in school to prepare the child for the conflicts of a psychological and social nature which are attendant upon adolescence.

Grounds for conflict between parents and children are somewhat varied. Some may be due to particular circumstances, as between children and a stepmother, or more commonly, between children and a stepfather. But in general conflicts centre round disputes concerning money, choice of a job, leaving home, and relations with the opposite sex.

Children from the ages of seven to fourteen who assist their parents do not receive wages. They may receive a shilling or less on Saturdays which they use to 'spree' themselves. The child may demand more and when it is not forthcoming a quarrel develops. But money disputes do not reach a serious stage until the child is earning money outside the home. Frequently the child will not make any definite contribution towards his keep and will spend all his earnings on himself. This inevitably leads to violent quarrelling which never really ceases until the child leaves home or a regular payment is arranged. The attitude of the child is 'What I earn I keep.' These money disputes concern both boys and girls. Typical jobs at the age of fourteen when they usually start work are as yard boys, and in domestic service.

Money disputes are therefore reciprocal. On the one side they come about through the parents not giving the child enough money; and on the other through the child not giving enough to the parents.

Some parents think that their children should try to better themselves. To this end they will advocate that the boy be apprenticed to a trade such as that of a carpenter, or the girl learn dressmaking. Both these occupations mean that there is a period when very little or nothing is earned by the child. The child may therefore feel that a job which offers more immediate returns is more worthwhile. If the child persists in this attitude the problem may be solved by his leaving home. The situation can also occur in the reverse sense, that is a child is forced to do work in which he thinks there is no future. The situation is relieved in the same way.

The actual leaving of home, for whatever reason, is apt to cause violent quarrels. The threatened absence of a member of the household, although he may only be making sporadic contributions, weakens the economic strength of the domestic group.

Another type of conflict between children and parents occurs in a household where the parents are not married, and the child has been persuaded of their immorality either at school or at church. The child will attempt to point out the error of their ways to the parents which leads to violent quarrelling. Amongst the cases of domestic groups which move from Faithful Concubinage to the Christian

Family many are due to the efforts of children who have altered their class status and are ashamed of their parents continuing to 'live in sin'.

At puberty both boys and girls begin to stay out late at night. This is the beginning of the period of sex experimentation. Parents often object to these nocturnal wanderings not so much on moral grounds as on account of the material fact that the child will be unfit for work the next day. The boy may be warned that it is too soon to start a sexual attachment because he is not yet making enough money, and if he does make a girl pregnant he may have to support her and the child. In some cases when this happens the pregnant girl, having no economic support, has to join the boy's domestic group.

Cases were found also of an exactly opposite kind. For example, a mother would exhort her daughter to find a man to keep her as she was becoming a burden on the family; 'It high time yo find a man to keep yo.' Such cases are of fairly frequent occurrence in all types of domestic groups except the Christian Family.

When the daughter gets 'stomach' – becomes pregnant – she may go through a period of disgrace, but finally the parents accept the inevitability of the situation. They may even be secretly proud that the girl has demonstrated her fecundity, or in the case of the boy, his virility. But the girl will have been warned about becoming pregnant as bringing another liability on the domestic group, so that initial conflict often occurs.

There are three ways in which the pregnant girl may be treated. If the father of the child is regarded as 'wutless', that is a ne'er-do-well, and so will make no provision for the girl, strong parental disapproval may be expressed. If the man is a good worker and likely to either support the girl or join the working strength of the domestic group, the parents will approve. In the case of a very poor domestic group the girl's intention to join the man's domestic group is approved.

Thus groups are expanded and new ones created according to individual action. But such action is in part determined by the economic and social framework of the society.

The Jamaican, however he may treat them, fundamentally loves children. He is not interested in whether they are born to a married couple or to an unmarried couple, or are the result of casual intercourse, but in the fact that the child is there. Complete social approval is given to having children. There is no social stigma attached to 'illegitimacy'. Only if a mother wilfully neglects her children may the question of who was the father arise, but this is rare.

A distinction has to be made between domestic groups in which a man is the head, and those in which a woman occupies this position. In general conflicts are fewer between a boy and the mother or maternal relatives in a house where the mother is the head. In these cases the boy feels a greater sense of responsibility towards his mother than he does in a group where the father is present. This responsibility is carried on throughout the lifetime of the mother or mother-substitute. Daughters in a maternal household tend to conflict with the mother, but the frequency of such conflicts is less marked than in the case of the boys in this type of household. In paternal households conflicts are more marked and more frequent.

One other cause of conflict is that mentioned above where a man, having made the daughter of a domestic group pregnant, moves into the household. If he has earning capacity he is made welcome, but if he is inclined to be shiftless his presence will be the cause of constant recrimination. In the first case he would be an economic asset, in the second a liability to a possibly already overburdened household.

All these conflicts appear to be due to the general instability of family groupings and to the fact that no special recognition is given by the society to the pubescent child. The child is not gently inducted into his or her new status as a man or a woman, but has to grope his or her way. This groping is the background of conflict.

The addition to a domestic group through the activities of either a son or a daughter has already been mentioned. The young girl is frequently ignorant of the responsibilities of rearing a family or living with a man. She inevitably turns to her mother-substitute for advice and knowledge. It has already been stated that the young generation is subjected to the ideas of two generations back, which can be seen in the persistence of Anansi stories which are learned from the grandmother rather than from the mother. Even if the daughter does not return to her own domestic group to live she will always seek her mother's aid in any important matter.

Christian Families tend to be both matrilocal and patrilocal.(2) The same could be said of Faithful Concubinage. But both the Keeper Family with its tendency to dissolve into the Maternal Family, and the Maternal Family itself are matrilocal. But these distinctions are not rigid, as so much depends upon particular circumstances. The influence of the father in A the Christian Family and in

B Faithful Concubinage is sufficient to account for patrilocality. Similarly, the influence of the mother or mother-substitute in the other categories results in matrilocality. Economic pressure as a factor must be discounted. In a patriarchal Christian Family economic factors may cause the pattern of the Maternal Family, that is, the married daughter may reside in her parents' home with her husband and children.

Another method of addition to a domestic group is through adoption. This is a widespread custom, though the legal forms requisite are seldom invoked. Cases commonly occur through the death of the mother. A mother will take a daughter's children into her home if they are not already living there. Adoption by a mother's sister is equally frequent. One encounters a great number of people who have been reared by a mother's sister. Often complete strangers will adopt children who take their fancy. Childless couples also adopt children, either those of relatives or of strangers.

Adoption serves the function in society of strengthening the domestic group by additions to its numbers. At the same time it allows scope for the development of the deep sentiment which Jamaicans attach to children.

NOTES AND REFERENCES

1. *Census of Jamaica*, 1943.
2. The rule by which a marital unit is set up near the family of the wife or the husband.

CHAPTER X

Kinship

ONE of the distinctive features of Jamaican lower class family life is the strong sense of kin which extends beyond the immediate family. In any domestic group taken at random it is probable that there will be adopted children, an aunt, some distant male relative, or perhaps someone who cannot claim any blood relationship whatsoever. If they are children they are treated as brothers and sisters by the biological siblings. The mother and father make no distinction between their own and the adopted children. The members of the group who do not possess a clearly defined position, as for example an uncle, are addressed as Coz, or Cousin.(1) To the child anyone who is older than himself is someone to whom deference must be paid as to his parents. Such a person will, if he or she is able, make a contribution to the upkeep of the household. They are treated as full members of the family in every sense.

A point to be emphasized is that the collateral relatives in a domestic group are found to be those of the mother far more often than those of the father. Thus in the Maternal Family, with the grandmother as its head, there may be grouped with her a number of her relatives of both sexes. In this type of family the sense of kin is more accentuated than in the other types.

In all matters connected with the family in Jamaica, except in the upper class, there appears to be both an unconscious and a conscious bias towards the maternal.

The sense of kin is extremely real but the actual knowledge of kin relationships is vague. All old women are addressed by both children and adults as 'granny'. While this in itself does not mean that the old woman is regarded as an actual grandmother, it shows the feeling of individuals towards the matriarchal female, and the desire to establish a bond with her. The equivalent form of address towards old men is far less frequently used.

The mother's or father's sisters, or women standing in their place, are known as 'aunty'. Uncle is similarly used for male relatives. But the bias is towards female relatives on the mother's side rather than towards those on the father's side. Very real bonds are established between children and these 'relatives' which persist throughout their lives. In a conversation about family matters there may be more references to 'aunty' than to father or mother.

Walking through a Jamaican town or village with an inhabitant, I found that a frequent form of address towards people was that of 'Coz'. In some cases the informant could establish a definite blood relationship with the person thus addressed, but in many others there was only the vaguest connexion. 'Coz' appears to be a term used for any relative of any generation irrespective of age, as well as for any person who is regarded as a relative though there is no blood connexion. Thus it will be used in addressing an uncle or an aunt as well as any actual young or old cousin to any degree of relationship, similarly the family friend enters into the same arc of relationship as the near or distant blood relative.

A definite distinction is made between the blood relatives, who may be addressed in terms of their actual position: aunt, uncle, or Coz, and the stranger with whom no actual relationship can be established and who is not connected with the family (i.e. a 'friend') in the way described above. This is evident in any family 'affair', whether it be a wake or a wedding – relationships are always stressed. Another distinction must be made between the complete stranger and the person who, although not a recognized connexion of a domestic group, is nevertheless on terms of intimacy with it. The latter may be, and often is, treated in the same way as the blood relative.

A contrast is provided by comparison with contemporary English village society. Owing to a variety of factors the relative isolation of the English village has tended to disappear. There is certainly not the same emphasis on the kin group as there is in Jamaica. A person walking through an English village might address people by their Christian names and be so addressed, but he would not use a special term which would suggest a real or imagined relationship as is the case in Jamaica.

In Jamaican lower class society there is a definite tendency to stress relationships between individuals. This it is suggested is because of the general social and economic insecurity which is reflected in the forms of the family. As the insecurity diminishes there is a corresponding waning of the stress. In the upper class there is less of kin feeling, though it is still much greater than in the equivalent class in

England. This economic interpretation of kinship does not discount the historical factor, but that which may have had an historical causation is now supported and controlled by the economic fabric of the society.

The ties of kinship are not confined to members of the lower class living in the island. The farm workers who went to the U.S.A. during the war illustrate this point very forcibly. The great majority sent home money and goods not only to their wives and concubines, but to their mothers and other relatives. A morning in any post office in the island reveals a large volume of correspondence taking place between Jamaicans and their relatives still working in the United States.

The interest in kin is not confined to one's own family. One of the chief pastimes in the island is the verbal investigation of other people's families. This may be compared with the practice which takes place in what is sometimes known as 'County' society in Britain, of identifying a particular family such as the Surrey Joneses, or the Warwickshire Smiths. It serves a very important purpose in Jamaican society as once the name can be connected with a particular locality, the family history can be sketched in and the identity of the stranger revealed. The stranger ceases to be a stranger once he is identified. This practice is by no means confined to the lower class.

Death also emphasizes the sense of kinship. In the West Indies burial must take place by law within twenty-four hours of death owing to the rapid decomposition of the body in the heat. As soon as the death occurs all the relatives within reach are notified. The relationship does not need to be a close one; even remote cousins are invited to attend the funeral. The funeral serves a dual purpose; it enables kin who have not met for years to renew bonds of friendship, and it serves to emphasize the loss by death to this group in the society. The everyday bonds of kinship are emphasized by the frequent visits made by members of a family to each other if they are separated, but the funeral enables those who are not able to meet frequently to re-establish the bonds of kinship.

The adjustment of the group to its loss by death takes the form of what is known as the wake.

The actual death-bed scene may be full of dramatic importance. The dying individual may go through what is known as 'confessing' – he demands the right to confess. He then starts to shout a torrent of obscenities and begins to tell the story of his life and of what other people have done to him.(2) All this may be of a very scandalous character as the person who confesses to enormities may have led an exemplary life outwardly. Some people maintain that it is Obeah which compels dying people to do this. The proof of this assertion to them is that only an Obeahman can stop the flow of the 'confession'.

The function of 'confession' appears to be in providing an outlet for the repressed feeling of the group. The audience although outwardly shocked at what it hears enjoys listening to stories which implicate its neighbours. The message of the individual is not confined to the room in which he is dying because he shouts it as loudly as he possibly can.

The corpse is specially treated before the funeral. The mouth is tied up and coffee grounds or the liquid itself are thrown over the back. Then the front part of the body is washed. The back of the corpse is not washed owing to the fact that it may break wind: 'If dead fart, you dead too.' A male corpse is dressed in his best suit, a bow tie is placed round the collar of the shirt, and the pockets of the suit are cut. This is done because when the dead become spirits they will fill their pockets with stones to throw at people. A female corpse is shrouded in her best frock or her wedding dress if it still exists.

If there is a small child in the household it is thrown three times over the coffin containing the body. But this is only done if the deceased was the father of the child. It is to prevent the father returning as a spirit to play with the child. Every ritual connected with the spirits is performed three times. One informant stated that this was because of the Christian Trinity.

The coffin is then brought out of the house into the yard. If the person was not popular or if the family is scared of his spirit a member of the family gets a broom and sweeps behind the coffin as it is carried out. This sweeps away the spirit and prevents it returning. It is never done by anyone who thinks well of the dead person's family. One must never look through one's legs at the coffin when it is passing as then the spirit of the dead person will be seen sitting underneath. If the ghost sees an individual it jumps on his or her neck and breaks it. But if someone particularly wants to see the dead man's ghost, perhaps for reasons of Obeah, he would take matter from the corner of a dog's eye and rub it on his own. Ghosts are visible to dogs and the faculty is transferred to the human eye in this manner.

In the yard the coffin is placed on two chairs with its head to the east. The body is always buried with its head facing towards the east. Then the minister or whoever is conducting the funeral gives a short address on the life of the deceased. A hymn is sung and the procession starts for the burial ground.

The coffin is carried by six or eight men. Everyone sings hymns as they proceed to the grave. The men carrying the coffin may start running; 'Look how him anxious to reach there.' Then everybody starts running. If the coffin is dropped it is because 'He [the deceased] don't want to go.' The body of a malevolent person may give the bearers a lot of trouble as according to the wickedness of the deceased the weight of the corpse will increase.

At the side of the grave the minister may address the mourners again after which the coffin is lowered into the grave.(3) Everyone then returns home in order to prepare for the 'wake'.

Throughout the island graves will be found in the yards of households. It is a practice confined to the country parts as opposed to the urban areas. It may be due to the fact that in slavery days the dead were buried on the estates. This applied to the masters as well as the slaves. On the other hand peasants still persist in the practice although there is adequate provision of cemeteries. From the above account it is seen that the coffin is *carried* to the burial ground. In many parts of the country the cemetery may be a considerable distance away from the dead person's dwelling. Informants gave this as a reason for the persistence of the practice of burial in the yard. The grave in the yard is generally covered by a stone slab or by loose stones. Washing is spread on top to dry or a meal is served on it. It may appear paradoxical that the family grave becomes so much a part of the household when one bears in mind the dread of spirits which exists in the island. The explanation may be that only those who were known to be good and who were loved are buried in the family yard. No Jamaican would choose to live in close proximity with the spirit of someone who had been notoriously wicked.

A wake starts when someone dies. Everyone is welcomed whether related to the deceased or not. This welcome extends beyond the circle of those who are known to the complete stranger. Many homeless people in urban areas wander about at night until they hear the sound of singing, and they discover a wake in progress. They know that they will be welcomed and given refreshment and somewhere to pass the night.

The wake may be described as a gathering of people in the house of the deceased. It consists of a core of relatives, and of many others who join with them. Hymns are sung, games played, stories told, and there is dancing while food and drinks are served. In very poor families each person brings his own food, but if they possibly can the family makes some attempt at provision. A master of ceremonies is generally in charge of proceedings. He may or may not be a relative. The festivities last for a period of nine days commencing on the night of the death with the corpse in the house. On the ninth night there is the biggest celebration of all which is known as 'Nint Night'.

The first night is passed in conversation. The next and subsequent nights cards and dominoes are played by the adults, and the children play such games as hide and seek in and out of the house. Stories, generally Anansi (i.e. of a folk character), may be told on these nights, though the practice seems to be dying out. Food and drink are served, but not in large quantities. It is only on the ninth night that the wake really comes into its own. The former nights can be regarded as marking time for this celebration. 'Nint Night' may start in the ordinary way with conversation. But soon the master of ceremonies takes charge and begins to organize the evening. If the musicians have arrived there is dancing. The music will consist of drums, a violin, and possibly a guitar and a cornet. The rhythm varies from the waltz to the mento (a typically West Indian rhythm), but the actual dance is that known as the 'Sets'. These are dances very much after the style of English country or barn dances. A man is surrounded by a circle of dancers. As they move round him he sings out what they are to do; 'Man, ketch your woman, wheel her', and so on. A variation is to have two people in the centre.

After a period of dancing hymns may be sung. These may not have any bearing on the fact that the family has suffered a bereavement. As is the custom with hymn singing anywhere in the island, outside of the orthodox churches, a leader speaks each line before it is sung. Hymn singing is often followed by the singing of obscene songs. These are sung by everyone including children who are generally unaware of their meaning.

The Bible may now be read to the accompaniment of interjections (Jesus! I'm saved) from the gathering. Then someone will begin an adulation of the deceased. This adulation is given whether the individual was a good man or a notorious rascal. This is followed by more hymns. People want to choose their own hymns but the M.C. or chairman will not always allow them to sing the hyms of their own choice. This causes discontent and comments such as 'Hear how him spoil me hymn.'

The proceedings continue in this fashion from dusk to daylight. This is so only for the 'Nint Night', on the other nights the wake may break up at one or two in the morning. About midnight or earlier food is brought out. It generally consists of a heavy meal of rice, peas, yams, and chicken. After this coffee and sweetmeats are handed round. Rum is drunk throughout the evening, though there are wakes at which no alcohol is consumed.

An individual can become known as a good master of ceremonies, or chairman, in which case his services are much sought after for wakes. His role can be quite onerous, however, as halfway through the evening people are inclined to become obstreperous.

Duppy or spirit catching takes place at some wakes. This is a ceremony designed to lay the spirit at rest for ever. The writer was unable to witness this as it is regarded with the greatest secrecy and only those who are connected with the dead in an intimate way can participate. An informant said that the close relatives go in procession to the graveside at midnight on the ninth night carrying lighted torches. The spirit is addressed and wrestled with until someone screams out: 'Me ketch him.' The captured spirit is then admonished and only let free on condition that it never haunts anyone.

The wake appears to serve a dual purpose. The household has suffered a loss in conjunction with the group. In order to mark the loss and at the same time to show that it is more apparent than real hymns are sung by the gathering and there is merriment and jollification. At the same time the whole serves as a rite of propitiation for the spirits, symbolized by the ceremony of catching the spirit. To the Jamaican the spirit world is part of the everyday world, only with this difference that an evil spirit can work greater evil than can a man. The obscenity can be regarded as an outlet for the fear implicit in any situation concerned with the spirits. The dancing serves to emphasize the normality of the occasion. The telling of Anansi stories is of definite ritual value in stressing the society's link with the past.

The wake used to be of great historical importance as it was one of the only means available for the slave to keep alive the traditions of his people. As in many Jamaican institutions there are elements in it of both African and European origin.(4)

The sense of kin is exemplified in the wake. But the feeling of kinship pervades the whole structure of the lower class. Within the framework of the domestic group and the vaguely defined kin group the individual finds satisfaction for his personal and social needs. The good and evil of every day are rationalized by the mechanism of his beliefs and practices. The resultant psychological type takes the form of a personality which, although emotionally largely dependent on his mother during youth, has no apparent homosexual tendencies.(5) But this personality is a prey to a series of anxieties arising out of the social and economic insecurities of life. These are combated by reliance on the kin group for economic and social aid. The frustrations of life due to colour are countered by indulgence in Obeah (witchcraft), and religious zeal. The lower class individual as a personality is volatile, unstable, and superficially, at least, easily satisfied emotionally.

NOTES AND REFERENCES

1. The term appears to be of English sixteenth-century origin.
2. Note the similarity with the practices of Moral Rearmament groups.
3. A minister may be of the orthodox kind, e.g., a Baptist, but there are so many different sectarian bodies that it is never difficult to obtain a minister or elder to officiate at a funeral.
4. Martha Beckwith, *Black Roadways*, Chapel Hill, 1929, pp. 78–84, gives an historical account of the wake, and as it was in her day (1919–24).
5. In its European manifestation male homosexuality is frequently associated with maternal dependence. See Michael Schofield, *Sociological Aspects of Homosexuality*, London, 1965, pp. 104–5.

CHAPTER XI

The Middle Class Family

THE transition from the lower to the middle class is marked by a modification of custom and behaviour rather than by an acute differentiation. The model of European society as exemplified in the upper class becomes the ideal. With this ideal there is an obvious tendency to condemn the behaviour of the common people as being primitive and uncivilized. Such condemnation does not necessarily lead to complete rejection of lower class customs. There is rejection of birth and child-rearing practices but not of lower class sexual habits.

As I have said there are two sections of the middle class. One prides itself upon a fairly strict Christian code of behaviour. The other tends towards a more lax sex code and in so doing draws upon characteristics of both the lower and the upper classes. It is necessary to emphasize that while the lower class attitudes towards the family and marriage are not to be regarded as a deviant or abnormality of Christian monogamy, it is Christian marriage which is the ideal in the middle class; therefore behaviour running counter to this can be regarded as abnormal.

In the discussion which follows the two sections of the middle class have been treated as one. The differences between the sections have been discussed above.

From the point of view of all the classes middle class status is determined mainly by occupation and behaviour. Colour itself is not a class determinant. Expressions such as 'Respectable black folk', 'Good brown people' are common in all classes to designate middle class families. It is true that the majority of the latter is brown as opposed to black, but individual black families may be respected more than individual brown families according to circumstances.

It is difficult to define exactly the values attached to different occupations. Working with one's hands does not in itself exclude an individual from the middle class. A fairly well-to-do peasant proprietor who works his land with his family and hired help would be considered middle class providing he conformed to the general behaviour of the class. On the other hand a man similarly situated who is not an assiduous churchgoer and who is known for casual connexions with women would not be so considered. But someone holding a minor position in the government service could behave in the same manner as the man in the latter case and yet not be rejected from the middle class. In other words the values of this class are such that manual labour must be excused by other characteristics of class behaviour such as churchgoing. Wealth will help to excuse non-class behaviour but only if it is obtained from a recognized class occupation.

'Family' is an important factor not only in determining the individual's class status but also in determining his status within the class. Examples were found of people who because they could trace a connexion with a well-known family were treated as members of the middle class though they themselves were living in a manner little different from that of the lower class. The authors of *Deep South* found similar instances among the white upper class in the American South.(1)

In Jamaica a marked characteristic of all classes is the interest taken in tracing the family connexions of other people. In the middle class this is a device which helps to determine status. In passing it is to be noted that the process of tracing ascendants must not be taken too far back as this introduces slavery as the source of origin. In this class the connexion with slavery as the source of origin is very rarely discussed. This is not so in the other classes.

If a family has achieved middle class status in the past it is difficult but not impossible for it to lose that status whatever its economic and occupational position may be in the present.

I have called the ability of the individual or family to move from one class to another social mobility. There is very little upward social mobility from the middle to the upper class. Here the barriers are colour and knowledge of the family. Money is a minor factor in the situation. Mobility from the lower class to the middle class is more frequent. Here the colour factor is of less importance but the individual or family must be prepared to subscribe to all the practices of the middle class. More is demanded from the aspirant to this class than from an established member of the middle class. As has already been stated there is little downward social mobility. Such cases as do occur are concerned with individuals who have not been long established in the middle class and through economic losses have had to change their mode of living.

Colour and 'family' are connected in the following way. Lighter coloured people can claim, though not openly, that they have a greater proportion of white blood in them than darker people. White blood denotes a superior social position. After emancipation, and even before, the ability to trace one's family back to a white man meant increased prestige. This is no longer done but such family pedigrees serve the function stated above.

Increased income provides the opportunity for better housing. A good home by middle class standards is a class prerequisite. The house will be as large as possible up to a maximum of nine or ten rooms. Furniture will be as costly as the family can afford. One or more servants will be employed. A nursemaid or 'nanny' is a middle class ideal which not all families can afford. The employment of a 'nanny' is in direct imitation of the upper class where there is one in every household which has children. Compared with the lower class wife the middle class wife has more time to devote to her children as she is rarely engaged in supporting her family. Thus the 'nanny' is an example of conspicuous waste. It is a badge of prestige.

Although a well-kept home is a class prerequisite it does not follow that all middle class homes are decent in appearance. Many are slovenly, but the majority strives towards the ideal of a 'good' home.

The birth of a middle class baby is not attended with any magical practices. It generally takes place in the hospital or in the home. There appears to be the same desire for children in this class as in the lower class. Ideas concerning birth control seem to be gaining ground, though not to any appreciable extent. The attitude towards the size of the family is governed by the religious – Biblical teaching. In practice a large family may be a hindrance to the parents. As the number of children increases so will the expenses connected with the children's education and placing in life. This is in contrast to the lower class, where an extra pair of hands can always be used in the 'field'.

In the early years parental love is at its height. There are few parents who correct their children physically. No attempts at reasoned arguments are made and the child is allowed to have its own way. 'He's only a child, he doesn't know any better.' This leads to a slower formation of living habits as compared to the swifter induction of the lower class child by means of beatings, etc.

This period of parental indulgence is followed in adolescence by a strong manifestation of authority. Adolescence is a time of danger for both sexes and the desires of the child must be curbed unless he or she is to form undesirable habits. Owing to his earlier upbringing the child is quite incapable of understanding the change of attitude; as a result intense conflicts are set up between the parents and the child.

The child cannot understand that although he used to be allowed to do more or less as he pleased he should now be compelled to adopt a particular form of restricted behaviour. The strictness of the parents is in part due to the facility with which both boys and girls can be 'led astray'. Before both the children and the parents there is the warning of the behaviour of the lower class.

The writer suggests that the psychological instability produced by this type of conflict in adolescence persists in the adult middle class Jamaican. It is more strongly marked in men than in women. It can be seen in a variety of ways, in the restlessness as regards occupation, emotional relationships, and in the preoccupation with gambling, etc.

The schooling of the child is much more regular than in the lower class. The child has adequate clothing and his or her assistance is not required in the home. Education serves the purpose of creating better economic and social opportunities for the individual (from a class point of view). Such opportunities are represented by employment in the minor grades of government service.(2)

Religion and churchgoing are important aspects of middle class family structure. The church is not only the dispenser of moral and social ideas, but it is also the centre of the middle class world. The church building itself is one of the few places where middle class people can mix on terms of apparent equality with members of the upper class.

The fundamental unit of the middle class family is the paternalistic, monogamous, Christian Family. It has certain features in common with its English counterpart. The difference lies in the emphasis placed on the position of the father. In Jamaica the family is centred in him. He is generally the sole support of the home. All authority is vested in him. He controls the group and guides its destinies. It is extremely rare for the wife to flout her husband's authority. In some instances the family extends to include collaterals of both the husband and the wife, or married sons and daughters with their children. In this extended family the authority of the father or grandfather is supreme.

The incidence of extended family groups is not frequent, but there are indications that the extended family occurred much more in the past than it does today. Evidence for this is found in references in the conversation of the older generation. Adoption helps to swell the range of the family, but it is not frequent, and usually occurs only when the death of the parents leaves the children orphans.

Funerals can be taken to indicate the strength of kin relationships in both the middle and upper classes.

Etiquette demands that on the death of a middle class person, all those who know the family should call before the funeral takes place. This is a custom fairly rigidly adhered to by middle class people. It is not so marked in the upper class where practice varies.

In all classes everyone who is at all connected by blood is expected to go to the funeral. But, and this illustrates the difference between the lower class and the other classes, everyone will go to a middle or upper class funeral who has the vaguest connexion with the deceased. The more important the individual, the longer will be the list of mourners published in the daily papers who followed the coffin to the grave. Some people even regard it as their duty to go to the funeral of anyone who was not completely unknown to them in his life. Prominent people cannot afford not to be seen at an important funeral. To be absent would cause their social prestige to fall. For these two classes the funeral is the expression not only of a personal loss, but of a loss to the groups in the society. In contrast, the lower class utilizes the funeral to re-emphasize the bonds of kin which is expressed in the institution of the wake.

Additions to the household which are treated on a non-familial level are made through the practice of keeping 'schoolgirls' or 'schoolboys'. This is similar to the Haitian custom of 'Ti-moune',(3) and is really a form of quasi-adoption. The child of peasant folk may be taken, at the intercession of his or her parents, by a middle class family. The child will live with the servant of the family, and is expected to make itself useful about the house and garden as well as attend school. In return it receives its keep and training in domestic work. Usually no wages are paid. The child may be received at the age of six or seven, and after five or six years it will either begin to receive wages or will leave to seek paid employment in another household. 'Schoolgirls' employed in this manner are much more frequent than 'schoolboys'.

The custom has a dual purpose. It enables the family to have the prestige of having a servant for a minimum expenditure, and at the same time it provides the lower class child with an avenue of employment, thus relieving the economic pressure on its domestic group. From references by middle class women, it appears that the custom used to be far more widespread than it is today.

The most important difference between the family groupings of the lower and middle classes is the almost complete absence, except fortuitously, of the maternal family in the middle class. This difference is emphasized by the power of the father in the middle class, and the more general subordination of women to men.

The Jamaican middle class is the equivalent of the late Victorian lower middle class. There is the same emphasis on the twin pillars of that society: religion and propriety. This similarity is a striking example of the perpetuation and survival of a form in a society when it is extinct in the parent society from which the former sprang. It is the writer's opinion that, as distinct from the lower class, where West African influences can be discovered, the middle class has been much more influenced by European forms.

The apparent stability of the family in this class has been vitiated in two ways. There is that section of the middle class which is not prepared to accept all the values and ideals of the class, particularly as regards religion and sexual behaviour. The majority of the class does not appear to be strong enough to ostracize this group, which is tacitly accepted by it. Research shows that the deviant group is increasing. Then there is also the factor of the younger generation which is just embarking on marriage. Owing to the economic difficulties of the times, and at the same time paradoxically enough the opening up of new avenues of employment, women are beginning to keep their jobs after marriage. This leads to a different orientation of life within the family group, and also to the diminution of the husband's authority.

The function of the family in this section of Jamaican society is not only to fulfil the purpose of a domestic group, but to act as an integrating force between the two social extremes of the lower and the upper classes. Whether it succeeds in this function is debatable, because its stability, in comparison with the upper and lower classes, is only apparent. The point to be emphasized is that the middle class believes that its own values and ideals represent the real values and ideals of Jamaican society as a whole although this belief is not common to the total society.

NOTES AND REFERENCES

1. A. Davis, B. B. Gardner and Mary R. Gardner, *Deep South*, Chicago, 1941, pp. 204–5.
2. See *Report of Middle Class Unemployment Committee*, Jamaica, 1941.
3. G. E. Simpson, 'Sexual and Familial Institutions in Northern Haiti', *American Anthropologist*, Vol. 49, No. 4.

CHAPTER XII

The Upper Class Family

It is necessary to re-emphasize here that the classification of 'lower class', 'middle class', and 'upper class' which has been adopted does not indicate a rigidity of division between the different classes in the island but is merely used for convenience in analysis. The distinction must be borne in mind that in the capital the European or white element forms the majority of the upper class. This is not true for the country as a whole where the upper class is of mixed composition with a preponderance of fair coloured people. The fair coloured people who are in the upper class in the country would form the upper layer of the middle class in the capital.

The behaviour of the upper class is governed to a great extent by European models. That is to say individuals attempt to guide their behaviour by what they think is the custom or practice in Britain. A typical instance of this is the wearing of dark clothes by men as formal dress. Ties with Britain are reinforced by the presence in the upper class population of people who have arrived comparatively recently from England or Scotland. Upper class people travel to Britain for vacations and return to regale their friends with stories of life at 'home'. The British bias is clearly indicated by such phrases as 'My Scottish grandmother', or 'My English grandfather', which are frequently heard. The psychological attitude is on the one hand to ape the European and on the other to deny both in ideas and in behaviour any connexion with the Negro and the slave past. This has given rise to the myth that this class has always been what it is, which is clearly not the case. The myth is accepted not only by the class itself but by the other classes. The two aspects of this attitude, the rejection of the Negro and the admiration of the white, are mutually reinforcing.

The Jamaican planters had a way of life which at its height tended to be magnificent. Jamaican memoirs are full of the luxury and grandeur of estate life. Their coloured and white kinsfolk have inherited or bought their lands but the magnificence vanished for ever with the abolition of the Sugar Protection Duties in the nineteenth century.

However, the planters' inheritance lingers on in the *dolce far niente* attitude of many of the upper class, and in certain customs which are gradually dying out.

The most important of these is that of the twin household with the 'outside' or 'love child'.

The ideal of the upper class in Jamaica is, as it is for the middle class, the Christian monogamous family. This is the unit of family structure, but it is a unit with variations. Marriage commands the greatest respect, but side by side with marriage is the custom of the twin household.

In the days of slavery the planter would choose a concubine from amongst the slaves on his estate. He would set up house for her adjacent to the 'great house' and provide for her and her children. In this custom lies the origin of many of the leading coloured families of Jamaica today. Needless to say their origin is never referred to in this way by members of the upper class. With the extinction of the old estate life at emancipation the custom underwent considerable modification. It survives today in the practice of both married and unmarried upper class men taking mistresses from the other two classes. A home may be created for the woman and the 'outside' children. There is a tendency today for the father to do less for the advancement of these children, but usually the 'outside' child will have all the advantages of education and career which the legitimate child has.

Today mistresses are obtained from the middle and lower classes; in the time of slavery it was a relationship between master and slave.

The attitude of the middle class towards this practice is not only one of tolerance but of actual approval. This is interesting as the twin household violates the canons of this class's sexual morality, and in addition the female partner is often drawn from its own class. The middle class girl who becomes the mistress of an upper class man is condemned, but the action of the man is approved. Members of the middle class who are questioned on this point say: 'But they've always behaved like that. So-and-so is a real Jamaican gentleman.' In one case an upper class fair man had a brown lower class woman as his mistress. He was unmarried and he paid for the upkeep of her home which he visited twice a week. Occasionally he was seen walking in the streets of the town with his mistress. Upper and middle class acquaintances would pretend not to see him. His conduct was never censured by anyone.

The explanation of the approval of this custom by the middle class may lie in the fact that such behaviour is attractive to it, but practice is hampered by the standards already adopted. Individuals who feel this may experience vicarious pleasure in knowing that upper class people can indulge in such behaviour. Condemnation of middle class men who imitate upper class behaviour, and of women who participate in twin households may be due to jealousy and the exposure of class weakness.

The attitudes of different members of the lower class may vary from open condemnation to approval: 'They just like us.' Condemnation is increasing with the increased prestige which the black man commands in Jamaica. Those who approve are generally people who firmly believe that their whole life is rooted in the goodwill of the upper class. Women who become mistresses of upper class men may be approved: 'She done well for herself', or condemned as betraying black solidarity.(1) This last attitude is found amongst the more politically advanced of the proletariat. There is no condemnation on moral or religious grounds.

The function of the twin household and the 'outside' child is dual. In the first place it represents to the upper class man an opportunity for sexual satisfaction outside marriage, as so many marriages are arranged on a basis of colour rather than of mutual attraction. Secondly 'outside' children help to swell the ranks of the upper class as the children eventually gravitate towards the class of the father. This pattern tends to increase with the social importance of the father.

The decline of the custom can be attributed to the increasing sexual accessibility of upper class women. This accessibility is due to the gradual deterioration of the sexual code of upper class women. The cause of the deterioration is the infiltration of contemporary European ideas together with the increased use of contraceptives.

The upper class in the country can be said to consist of planters and the highest grade of government officials together with such professional men as there may be in a particular parish. It is the equivalent of what is known as 'County' society in England. Other factors being equal, colour is the real determinant of membership of this class. It is mostly composed of white, fair, and a few brown individuals.

The ritual concerned with the birth of children is characteristic of the upper class. Money takes the place that magic does in the lower class birth. The pregnant mother is sent to the capital where admission has been sought to the most expensive private nursing home in the island which is patronized by the European element. To have her baby there is a mark of prestige for the mother and consolidates her position in the upper class. To have her baby in the local hospital or at home would demonstrate a lack of means incompatible with class status. There are many cases where a great economic sacrifice has been made in order to have the child born in an expensive nursing home.

The rearing of the upper class child has a degree of similarity with that of the lower class child. The parents in both classes tend towards excessive indulgence. But whereas in the lower group this indulgence is modified by the time the child grows up, in the upper class this indulgence may persist throughout the lifetime of the child at home.

The nanny usurps the function of the mother. The mother is preoccupied with duties of a social nature and has little time to devote to the child except for a few months after its birth. The nanny may be an efficient woman, but she is usually also an ignorant woman. The result is that during a very important formative period of the child's life it is very much influenced by ideas of the lower class. In some cases the *rapport* established between the nanny and the child may be more intense than that between the mother and the child. Many adults speak affectionately of their former nannies, and in times of trouble will assist them financially. The nannies are drawn from what is termed the 'respectable element' of the lower class. These women serve as a link between the two class extremes of the society. The understanding gained by the upper class child of the lower class is never entirely lost in later life however harsh his public attitude may be towards the latter.

Every afternoon in the town there is a parade of nannies with their upper class charges. The mothers are preoccupied with tennis, bridge, or cocktails at this time. It is only on very special occasions that a mother will accompany an infant out of doors when it is at the perambulator stage. This is in complete contrast to the other classes where the women are seen everywhere with their children. This dislike of public demonstration of motherhood may be due to the unconscious reaction to the excessive display of the lower class in this matter. Despite this, upper class pregnant women will appear in public until the eighth month which is contrary to the practice in the

United States where upper class women who are pregnant make infrequent public appearances.

At about the age of six the child begins to leave the care of the nanny. Its afternoons are spent at the Tennis Club which is the focus of the social life of the upper class. It plays unobtrusively in the background while the mother is engaged in gossip, bridge, or tennis.

Children's parties at a private house may transgress class and colour lines between the upper and the middle classes. Cases were observed where middle class fair children were invited to upper class children's parties when the mothers were not on visiting terms. Such behaviour does not take place in adolescence when its occurrence might lead to romantic attachments between the sexes. The abrupt change in the parental attitude towards class differences which occurs at the child's adolescence helps to crystallize the younger upper class Jamaican's attitude towards the middle class.

Eating habits indicate the degree to which children are indulged by the parents. The majority of children in the upper class households in the town refuse to eat properly. They will put on a pantomime of repugnance at every meal and will have to be coaxed and cosseted before touching the food. Parents will rarely attempt to use the threat of punishment to coerce the child; the nanny is expected to deal with the situation. This is the only time during the day when the child can command the full attention of the mother, and he or she makes the utmost use of it.(2)

At about eight years of age the child is sent to boarding school in the capital or elsewhere. There he or she meets its fellows and some middle class children. School experience tends to confirm the knowledge already picked up at home – that his or her colour and social position will always command respect in Jamaican society. There is no colour bar in the schools, but the child soon discovers that he is at an advantage as for instance compared with the wealthy black child.

Boarding school and the fact that according to the wealth of the parents the child can choose any career it likes produce less conflict between the parents and children. Such conflicts as do occur are concerned with extravagant expenditure and the use of the family car, rather than with leaving home and the kind of career to be chosen.

The upper class child or adult has in his social situation something which is lacking in the other classes. He knows that by virtue of his colour not only will he be welcomed everywhere but that in itself his colour commands respect. Money will enable him to further his education abroad and any career is open to him. An individual of this class may lose his money, but he cannot lose his colour or class position. In other words he will still be entitled to and will receive the respect due to an upper class person although he may not have the money which usually goes with that position. This results in a surety about life which amounts almost to arrogance. This is in marked contrast to the other classes where there is so much more social and economic insecurity.

As with the middle class, there is almost a total absence of maternal family groupings. The family is governed by the father. In the recent past patriarchal family groups dominated by the grandfather were common. Today they occur comparatively rarely. The extended family comes into being only on certain special occasions such as weddings and funerals, or if a domestic crisis arises. Ascendants and collaterals are recognized but it is nothing much beyond simple recognition. Emphasis is laid upon the 'Family' itself. The habit of tracing family connexions is not so marked as it is in the middle class. Obviously there is less necessity for this as status is already determined. There is an immense pride in being of 'good' family. If one's family is not as 'good' as it might be colour and money help to overcome this disadvantage.

Family attitudes in the upper class are very different from those in the other classes. Stemming from assurance in the individual himself there is much less concern with kin and kin groupings. The contemporary English upper middle class family, if certain essential differences such as colour qualifications are taken into consideration, represents the equivalent of the Jamaican upper class family.

Social groupings within the class may take the form of cliques arranged according to colour and interests. These cliques are by no means permanent but may come into being for a temporary purpose as during a period of intense bridge playing. Their existence involves a considerable amount of backbiting and criticism about other members of the upper class who are not members of the particular clique. A clique may be determined by income; for example the wealthy members of the upper class tend to gravitate towards each other. But here as in other activities colour is a strong determinant in the actual composition of a clique.

Religion does not play the important part it does in middle class society. The great majority of the upper class are members of the

Anglican Church. There are a few Roman Catholics, but rarely if ever does the individual belong to any other denomination. 'Good' works of the church are supported financially, but if the colour of the parson is 'wrong' it may mean that upper class parishioners are absent from church. There is a conventional acceptance of the teaching of the Anglican Church in preference to others but there is no zeal for religion as such in the manner in which it is found in the other classes.

An analysis of the upper class family shows that while it serves the elementary and fundamental purposes of the family or domestic group its function in the wider sense is more limited than is the case in the other classes. The upper class individual is less dependent upon the kin group for success or failure in the society, and consequently such relationships are not stressed to the extent which they are in the lower class where the reverse is true. The individual is acutely conscious of his position in the society, and is aware of his superiority to other classes and colours. Class education and training emphasize class solidarity. The upper class is the nearest approach to the European ideal in the total society. The class function, therefore, becomes one of representing this ideal to the whole society.

NOTES AND REFERENCES

1. A. Davis, B. B. Gardner and Mary B. Gardner, *Deep South*, Chicago, 1941, pp. 31–9.
2. One upper class mother explained the refusal of children to eat unless coaxed by saying that it was because so many of them had worms.

The Tourists' Jamaica. *Photo:* Jamaica Tourist Board

Bauxite mining. *Photo:* Jamaica Tourist Board

CHAPTER XIII

Conclusions

PROFESSOR A. R. RADCLIFFE BROWN has used the terms eunomia and disnomia to describe the degree of integration or balance which obtains in a given society. All societies must have some measure of eunomia in order to exist, but having regard to the inconsistencies and contradictions of human behaviour there can be no such thing as complete eunomia. Similarly, complete disnomia is difficult to conceive as such a state implies an entire lack of order in which a society could not exist.

This being so it follows that in using such terms to describe a particular society they can only be used in a relative sense. Thus in the light of the foregoing analysis it is possible to describe Jamaica as a disnomic society when compared with Britain, and Britain as relatively eunomic when compared with Jamaica.

That eunomic factors exist in Jamaica is clear from the material presented, but the total picture is one of disnomia.

Bounded by the framework of poverty the majority of Jamaicans has few channels of expression open to them. Social frustration is the hallmark of that poverty. The domestic groupings, which are the result in part of the social heritage of slavery and in part of the desire to achieve a balance lacking in the society as a whole, are the basis of the social structure. Colour distinctions and their concomitant prejudices are a major factor increasing tensions which add to the general disnomia.

The class structure invites comparison with Britain. There is a similar social stratification but with the important difference that class is determined not only by education and wealth, but by colour. The situation in some parts of the United States where coloured people are relegated to an inferior social position by law and custom does not obtain in the island. In Caribbean society as a whole colour by itself can determine an individual's position in the social hierarchy. However, that position may be and often is affected by economic wealth. Thus the possession of 'bad' colour can be offset to some degree by the acquisition of wealth. As has already been pointed out this does not lead to complete social acceptance by fair skinned groups, but to increased prestige for the individual and a modified acceptance. This is a continuous process. In recent years it has been amplified and extended through economic changes and the pressure of political events.

The use of the class divisions upper, middle, and lower, is a necessary methodological device and does not indicate the actual divisions in the society. There is a gradation of class which largely depends upon subtleties of colour and which does not yield readily to analysis. As the class ladder is ascended from lower to upper there is a steady diminution of family and kin feeling. In the lower class the individual is dependent to a great extent upon the kin group for his social and emotional security. This in itself is the result of poverty and colour which deprive him of a wider field of social opportunity. At the other extreme are the members of the upper class who, although aware of colour disadvantages in a more subtle form, are not confined by poverty so that social and emotional dependence express themselves in a wider field. Situated in between the middle class possesses attributes of both the other classes. Here the family is in an essentially fluid state responsive to pressure from both above and below. Colour, as a disintegrative factor, assumes its greatest importance in this class.

The term 'domestic group' was adopted to describe the lower class familial groupings, as it was felt that the more usual term of 'family' which describes the unit of father, mother, and children, both biological and socially ascribed, did not cover certain manifestations of family life in this class, such as that of the maternal or grandmother domestic group in which the father is absent. It also avoids the implication of marriage, often absent in Jamaican households, which exists in the use of the word 'family'. I have tried to show that these domestic groups satisfy the needs of the elementary biological family, and also the larger social needs implicit in the framework of poverty.

In the middle and upper classes the family approximates to the contemporary English family. The demands of these groups are met by similar forms. The different response of the society, according to the class in question, is determined in part by the difference in economic level. There is no necessity in the middle and upper classes for a family structure which caters for the majority of the social needs of the individual, as satisfaction for those needs is supplied from outside the family. The social horizon of these groups extends beyond familial relationships, whereas in the lower class it is largely confined within them.

I have suggested that Jamaican society is disnomic. This cannot be interpreted to mean that the individual forms of the social structure are unbalanced. In fact the contrary is the case. The structure of domestic and family groupings is itself balanced. But the existence of such types of familial associations in conjunction with poverty and colour create disnomia in the total society. The forms of the family are balanced in themselves, but their existence is symptomatic of disnomia in the society as a whole. A comparable society would be that of an occupied European country during the war. The members of the Jewish community in Holland during the German occupation are a case in point. Oppressed and persecuted, they created a definite behaviour pattern which from a structural point of view was in essence stable. Yet the existence of such patterns was symptomatic of the disnomia inherent in Dutch society at that time.

Much has been said in Jamaica and elsewhere of the stigma of 'illegitimacy'. It is regarded as an index or symptom of disorganization in the society. This is not my opinion. There appears to be a fundamental error in mistaking the overall disnomia of the society for internal structural disorganization. The error on the part of observers springs from the confusion, in the case of the lower class, of substituting the ideal of Christian monogamous marriage for the ideal of that class. That is to say in assessing the lower class forms of the family the norm is held to be Christian monogamous marriage. Children of unions not within that category are held to be illegitimate, and such unions are regarded as deviants from the norm of Christian monogamy. The illegitimacy rate is then used as an index of social disorganization. As has been shown the norm for the majority of the Jamaican lower class is not Christian monogamy. That being so, the use of illegitimacy as an index of disorganization can only obscure the real nature of the problem.(1)

An important characteristic of the lower class domestic groups is the dependence on the mother or mother-substitute. This is found in its most conspicuous form in the maternal or grandmother groups. The usual period of maternal dependence is enlarged from that of childhood to include the greater part of adult life. The important place given to the mother by members of the lower class is further intensified by the relatively greater freedom possessed by women in this class, as evinced by the institutions of Faithful Concubinage and the Maternal Family. A daughter can look for protection and care for herself and her children to the latter group. A son will tend to identify his mother with the functions of the father for when the latter is present there is equality between the man and the woman. Further evidence of the independence of women, which tends to crystallize in the functions of a father-substitute, is seen in the profession of the 'higgler' described above. The psychological implications of this type of family situation cannot be overlooked.

Child-rearing techniques vary from class to class. In the lower class the emphasis upon folklore is coupled with both indulgence and severity towards the child. The child is in many instances, through the influence of the maternal grandmother, brought up in the ideas and traditions of two generations before. In the middle and upper classes folklore is largely dispensed with, but the indulgence-severity attitudes persist. In all classes children up to adolescence are regarded as an unmixed blessing to be cared for and cherished. This feeling is presented in its most definite form, despite the comparatively high incidence of cruelty, in the lower class domestic groups.

Adoption serves as a means of increasing the strength of a kin group. Its high incidence in the lower class illustrates the desire of people to possess children. There may be an economic motive concerned as dependence in childhood may give place to assistance at adolescence. This, however, would not be sufficient to explain the very real desire of men and women to have children even in the most appalling circumstances. The roots of this attitude possibly lie in the persistence of the slave tradition which encouraged fecundity, and the acceptance of fundamentalist Christian theology with its emphasis on the Old Testament. Quotations from the Bible are familiar to even the most illiterate of peasants. For a woman to have a child as the result of casual intercourse does not create social disapproval; it is regarded by lower class society as a mark of fertility – as showing that she is capable of contributing to the strength of the group. Parents have an ambivalent attitude which in most cases crystallizes into approval, particularly if the man responsible can be brought into the domestic group. Conflicts between children and parents are much more likely to occur with boys than with girls, and are caused primarily by the choice of work.

In the middle and upper class families, which possess elements of both the Victorian and contemporary English family, there are heavy sanctions for women against any departure from the ideal of

Christian monogamy. Approval is given to the fathers and their 'outside' children, but is withheld from the mothers whatever class they may come from. Exceptions to this 'paternal' approval are found in a section of the middle class. Adoption is practised, but not to the extent apparent in the lower class. There is less necessity for it as the kin groups are weaker, and do not serve the same important functions as in the latter class. Children are regarded as fulfilling the purpose of marriage, but approval is not given to having a child for its own sake. Parent-child conflicts are not as intense in these groups as defection (through choice of a career, etc.) does not disturb the balance of the unit as it may do in the lower class. Also the practice of sending children to boarding school in the upper class and the wealthier section of the middle class tends to lessen contact and so reduce conflict, particularly at the period of adolescence when most conflicts are liable to occur.

The distinction between the lower class domestic groups on the one hand, and the upper and middle class families on the other, is even more clearly seen in death customs. For the lower class the death of a member of the group is not only a loss to the immediate domestic group, but a loss to the whole community. This loss is emphasized in the custom of the wake in which participants are drawn from both inside and outside the domestic and kin groups. The wake is a means of establishing the community's loss and at the same time of emphasizing the continuity between the dead and the living. The domestic group becomes identified with the community. By contrast in the other classes death is much more the private concern of the particular family. Funerals attract a large attendance of non-relatives, but that is essentially a public demonstration of prestige which increases as the class ladder is ascended rather than the fusion of public and private sentiment which is the characteristic of the wake.

Attitude and behaviour towards youthful sex relationships are dependent upon the forms of the family. Where the ideal unit of family structure is the Christian monogamous family there is generally found active disapproval of female extra-marital behaviour. This disapproval is extended to male infidelity in one section of the middle class. Youths and men are allowed to deviate from the ideal in order to gain sex experience, but with marriage they are expected to 'settle down'. Women who deviate are subject to extreme disapproval in the form of ostracism. In the lower class domestic groups where the ideal is very different and the emphasis is upon children for their own sake the attitude towards such sex relationships is characterized by tolerance.

Sexual freedom both during the youthful period of experimentation and later is extended to both sexes. The forms of the family permit this attitude which by middle and upper class standards is very lax. Sexual freedom within these groups does not affect the family structure as it would in the other classes. Because of the essentially fluid nature of the structure there is not the same necessity for the institutionalization of extra-marital behaviour in the form of concubinage and the 'outside' child, as there is in the upper and middle classes.

The family can be regarded as one of the main cultural foci of the society. But as the class ladder is ascended the intensity of its function decreases. This means that in the lower class there is an emphasis upon the domestic group and its allied kin groupings, which springs from the very nature of the social structure of that class; whereas in the middle class there is a shift of emphasis to other foci, such as colour. Then as the social horizon is gradually enlarged with increased income and social prestige appertaining to colour there is a steady diminution of emphasis until the upper class family begins to occupy the position of the middle and upper class family in England, and the shift of emphasis is complete.

The economy of the island is still largely governed by the heritage of the past. Its main characteristic is the great inequality between the extreme poverty of the majority of the people, and the wealth of the few. The figures of earnings embodied in the text demonstrate the poverty stricken existence of the average Jamaican.

Attempts have been made by successive administrations to deal with the problems accruing from the acute impoverishment of the people. Land settlement in its modern form has done something to give the peasant a poverty-free basis, but the happy picture delineated by Lord Olivier is no longer true.(2) Today the government is confronted with an enormous number of unemployed and a population which is increasing at the rate of between 1½ per cent and 2 per cent per annum.(3) The creation of new industries such as bauxite mining, the assistance of the Colonial Development and Welfare fund, and the development of the tourist trade may all help to change the situation radically. But the Jamaican peasant with his somewhat primitive methods of agriculture remains the symbol of the poverty of the island. With the restoration of world sugar production to normal (e.g. beet sugar areas in Europe, and sugar areas in the East Endies) sugar production in Jamaica will eventually revert to its low pre-war level. The banana is not sufficient on its own to stabilize the economy. The island's economy must become more diversified if it is to become more balanced.

New ways of solving the problem of chronic poverty will have to be devised. The effect of poverty on the functioning of the social structure cannot be overestimated. In my opinion the creation of better housing and the installation of electric light might have a profound effect on the life of the Jamaican lower class. Sex habits and customs fostered by overcrowding might undergo a considerable modification in the face of more space and light.

The great inequality of wealth does not in itself create the forms of the social structure, but it is the essential background of those forms and helps to crystallize the habits of years into unshakeable custom. It is the most general symptom of the disnomia inherent in the society.

Colour is a phenomenon peculiar to this type of 'colonial' society. Originating in the particular historical circumstances of Jamaica it dominates the springs of social action in the middle and upper classes and influences the behaviour of the lower class.

The black lower class individual is not only bound by his poverty but is frustrated by the knowledge that if he does overcome the barriers of poverty social frustration is inevitable as a result of his colour. In English society it is possible for a man to rise (with economic success) from a working class origin to membership of a higher class providing care is taken to disguise that origin by such means as the elimination of a socially undesirable accent and the acquisition of the manners of the superior class. I suggest that because of this freedom of class mobility there will be little or none of the particular type of social frustration found in Jamaica.

The middle and upper classes with their complicated system of 'colour' values exhibit a higher degree of frustration than the lower class. To these classes poverty is not a problem. But anxiety regarding social position which is dependent on colour produces a greater conflict in members of the two upper classes than it does in black members of the lower class. The social horizon of the individual in this class is severely limited as are his anxieties which take a simple if dominant form. The upper or middle class individual has an infinitely wider social horizon, but it is attended by a complex of anxieties which create more acute conflicts than are possible in the lower class. The occupational disease of the former classes may be said to be colour.

These conflicts have issued in the form of a distinct personality type. This personality type signifies the contradictions and tensions of Jamaican society.(4)

The writer has used the term 'white bias' to describe one of the chief psychological motivations in the society. Obviously the colour of an individual is a biological inheritance which is not subject to change. 'Colour' as interpreted in Jamaica consists in the evaluation of data concerned not only with actual skin colour, but with features, hair formation, and skin texture. The further removed an individual is from the African and the nearer to the European ideal, the greater his social prestige. This is a manifestation which overleaps class barriers and is found throughout the society. The widespread male preference for a mate of 'better' colour than himself is evidence of its class-wide incidence. But friction about colour does not take place only within the family, where it may be extremely acute, but is carried into the public sphere where it is the major determinant of social distance between people.

Families may be divided along colour lines and so disunity be created. If the individual could find compensation for this type of frustration in public life, the personality type would be considerably modified. As it is, in the public sphere there is even greater frustration. The question of the choice of a career, promotion from an existing job, public and private acceptance by other people, are all profoundly affected by the colour of an individual. He finds that the tensions inside a family group are intensified tremendously outside that group. The result is mental irresolution and uncertainty whose symptoms are the exhibition of conceit and arrogance which in reality conceal a profound sense of insecurity.

Colour is the major determinant of social position and is the basis of middle and upper class frustrations. In fact colour can be said to pose the whole problem of 'cultural' values in the Caribbean.

Culture contact between the African and the European has not, in Jamaica, followed the lines of detribalization. The detribalization process was already initiated with the arrival of the first slaves in Jamaica. A unique pattern is discerned. The amalgam of West African tribes was, in the ensuing historical process, deprived of the greater part of its African culture. The emergence of a coloured class, the result of illicit unions between black and white, which took over the European values of the planter was permanently in front of the Negro. Emancipation did not lead to the re-establishment of African values, but to the intensified adoption of European values.

That is not to suggest that contemporary Jamaica does not exhibit Africanisms in its culture, but that the upper and middle classes have succeeded in denigrating things African to such an extent that the individual of whatever class feels that anything African is to be despised. Even the black lower class individuals will voice their disapproval of black or 'Naygur' things. The fact that Obeah and Pocomania flourish is in part historical accident, and in part the response to the necessity for an emotional and social outlet. That participation in these activities has little prestige value in the society as a whole is shown by the shamefaced attitude of devotees towards them.

The barrier to complete assimilation of European cultural values is contained in 'colour' itself. The physical fact of colour symbolizes to the individual that there can never be complete identification with the superior culture. That is a measure of the frustration. Government at the highest level, orthodox religion, education, are all associated with white superiority. The efforts to revolt against the 'white bias' are checked by the constant reinforcements in the form of ideas and individuals which strengthen the white and quasi-white groups.

But the fact that political events have created an almost all-black legislature has done a great deal to advance black prestige. However, colour manifestations are extremely complex. While many people would be prepared to admit colour equality at the public level the same admission in private life and personal relations raises different problems.

Political events in the future may intensify colour feeling, which, with the growth of a black middle and upper class, will tend to oust the white and fair coloured people from their long-held position of social superiority. But whether even that would produce the extinction of the 'white bias' in the society is debatable.

The frustrations of poverty and colour lead in the lower class to the demand for a social and religious outlet. The orthodox churches while serving an important function in the society do not lend themselves to this. The demand is filled by Pocomania on the group level, and by Obeah on the private or personal level.

Pocomania and other cult practices allow the individual full scope to express himself. He can, through the mechanism of the trance, attain a degree of identification with the spirits and so with superordinate powers which are denied him in his daily life. It offers him compensation for the hardness and aridity of his existence. Through this means he can express himself socially and become someone with a sense of importance. This in part explains the hold which Pocomania has on the people. In the rites and ceremonies of the cult the material world is held to be of little account. The emphasis is upon the supernatural world where 'Quashie' (the Jamaican man in the street) comes into his own. The individual can escape from the frustrations of everyday life and become, according to the teaching of Pocomania, part of a greater and more powerful spiritual world in which poverty and colour do not exist.(5)

The orthodox churches attempt to convey the same message but their material context or social background is a contradiction of this message. The leaders of Pocomania, unlike those of the latter churches, suffer the same humiliations and frustrations as 'Quashie'.

The trance might be construed as a development of early revivalist practices in Europe, but on the other hand it seems to have more in common with West African forms of the trance. This is certainly true in Haiti and Trinidad.(6) Its Jamaican adaptation as a vehicle of individual expression is of great importance for both participants and onlookers.

Obeah or witchcraft offers power over events. It is essentially magical and, as opposed to Pocomania, hidden and secret. It promises that the problems of daily life can be overcome for the benefit of the individual. Its role can be seen as offering to the Jamaican peasant an avenue for obtaining redress through magic against a hostile world.

Historically it is of importance as a cultural focus. Under slavery the Negro was unable to perpetuate his original culture. Obeah was the only cultural manifestation which survived as a whole in the period of cultural isolation. Its strength today can be explained in terms of its historical role as a rallying point for rebellion. While slavery has vanished the condition of the Jamaican peasantry is such that the invocation of supernatural powers is necessary in order to compensate for the social frustrations. The fact that no real attempt was made until recently to improve the condition of the lower class brings out the importance of the functions of Obeah.

This neglect taken in conjunction with other factors has created a strong messianic tradition in Jamaica. The messiah appears in both the political sphere – Marcus Garvey is an example – and the religious sphere: Bedward. The role of the messiah in both these spheres is the same, to promise salvation in the face of physical and social realities of insuperable severity without the expenditure of any real effort on the part of the people.

Pocomania upholds this tradition in that it produces local saviours. Its leaders represent the messianic tradition, and their office provides a channel for the expression of leadership amongst the people. Thus it acts as a compensation for the general frustration in the society. It offers a means of expression which is denied by other institutions, and at the same time by its very nature it can be regarded as a symptom of disnomia.

The leaders of the cult groups are not a class apart and their way of life is in no way different from that of the peasant or urban worker. A Pocomania leader will preach and inveigh against the sins of the flesh which his congregation enjoys, while he himself will be 'sinning' with one or more of the female initiates of his group.

To sum up; the hypothesis put forward is that Jamaican society is in a state of disnomia and that the major causes of this disnomia are poverty and colour. The family structure betrays the influence of poverty and is the result of a response to the general social situation. This structure is not itself disorganized, but exhibits a remarkable consistency and definiteness of pattern within its framework. Pocomania can be regarded as a symptom of disnomia and at the same time as a response to frustrations in the society. Jamaican personality, the product of a unique complex of factors concerned with colour, typifies the general social instability.

A consideration of Jamaican society raises problems connected not only with other parts of the Caribbean, but with British colonies as a whole wherever there has been conflict between white and black peoples. The uniqueness of the Jamaican situation lies in the fact that there has been both a conscious and an unconscious attempt on the part of many people to destroy the original culture of the great majority of the inhabitants, a process which has been all too successful.

Assimilation of European culture for the middle and upper classes has been successful, but only at the expense of producing a personality type which demonstrates a profound insecurity. The problem for the lower class in the elaboration of its institutions has been to endeavour to find avenues of expression denied it by the greater society. In the last analysis the attempt has been successful, and the resultant syncretism of thought and practice is the hallmark of Jamaican culture.

That the unbalanced state of the society should be rectified is implicit in the preceding analysis. This can only be achieved by the creation of a balanced economy and the eradication of the 'white bias' from the society by propaganda and education.

No society is static, and the forms described are constantly undergoing a process of modification and change. What has been attempted is a tentative analysis of certain of those forms separated from the continuum which is Jamaican society.

NOTES AND REFERENCES

1. A similar problem occurs in Sweden, Alva Myrdal in *Nation and Family*, London, 1945, pp. 40–1, that 'The lack of a registered ceremony is not always to be interpreted as immorality.'
2. Lord Olivier, *Jamaica : The Blessed Island*, London, 1936, pp. 435–7.
3. *Report of the Royal West India Commission*, H.M.S.O., London, 1945.
4. For a discussion of the wider implications of this personality type see E. E. Stonquist, *The Marginal Man*, N.Y., 1947, pp. 139–59, also Madeleine Kerr, *Personality and Conflict in Jamaica*, revised edition, Jamaica, 1963, pp. 165–74.
5. Cf. the function of religion in the American South in J. Dollard, *Caste and Class in a Southern Town*, N.Y., 1957, pp. 248–9.
6. A. Metraux, *Voodoo in Haiti*, London, 1959, pp. 120–47, and M. J. Herskovits, *Trinidad Village*, N.Y., 1947, pp. 309, 336–9.

CHAPTER XIV

Reassessment

DESPITE the great changes which have occurred in Jamaican society in the last twenty years I would maintain that my original hypothesis of the 'white bias' in the society is still operative. That is to say although the structure of colour-class relationships has undergone what appears to be considerable modification nevertheless the basic orientation of the society towards a European ideal remains. The essential contradiction of a society in which 90 per cent of the population is of non-European origin yet which models itself on a European ideal is as powerful as ever. The parallel with the Negro-American is of some significance. In the U.S.A. of Freedom Marchers and the Black Muslims the sale of hair-straightening devices and whitening creams is higher than ever before.

Political independence has produced a number of overt changes in the public sector. The structure of government no longer permits the white ex-patriate to dominate his black or coloured colleagues. The titular head of state – the governor-general – is a black man. Parties at King's House, long the cherished preserve of the white and fair coloured, are open to all. Black or dark men have even been appointed to the office of *Custos*(1) which until very recently was the prerogative of the white or near white. To the uninitiated these represent a radical transformation. The reality of the situation, it is suggested, is somewhat different.

One of the anomalies of the Jamaican situation is the non-appearance of black leadership. Both political parties rely on the support of the black masses but no black individual has dominated either. An analogy with the public school leadership of the British Labour Party would not appear to be valid. In Britain the working class lad can shed his origins as he advances on the ladder of politics. In Jamaica, precisely because of the 'white bias', blackness connotes an inherent incapacity. This is not merely the view of the traditionally favoured, brown, middle class, but of all sections of the community.

An opinion which is found amongst all classes and colours in relation to the absence of black leadership is that the fair and brown are more capable of representing Jamaica either at home or abroad. A common rationalization was that as it was a white world it is easier for the fair Jamaican to elicit support and sympathy abroad. If taxed with the fact that African countries did not apparently experience this disability the informant was likely to deny that Jamaica was an African society. It is a fact that at this time (1967), the Jamaican ambassadors to Washington and London are members of the white or fair coloured group. For the mass of Jamaicans the equation between fair colouring and education and ability is still a valid one. The advantages in terms of education, of the coloured middle classes are still operative. The structure of the Jamaican educational system has favoured this. It is quite otherwise in Barbados where, in the absence of a privileged coloured group, the mass of black people have enjoyed the best educational system in the British Caribbean. The result has been that Barbadians are prominent in the field of education all over the West Indies.

Before discussing in detail what might be described as Jamaica's search for identity, that is the whole complex struggle of Africa and Europe in the minds of people, it is useful to look at other changes which have occurred in the last twenty years.

In the field of employment and economic opportunity the expanding economy has had a number of effects. To be black in the 'fifties, whether one had education or not, was to experience considerable difficulty in obtaining satisfactory employment. This was particularly true of the black middle class. Traditionally prestige occupations, such as banking and clerking, operated a clandestine colour bar. It was, as we have said, virtually impossible for a black girl to obtain a post in a bank or as a sales clerk. In Kingston today this still appears to obtain with relation to most banks and stores. In country districts, however, banks employ dark counter staff which would have been unthinkable only a few years ago. This is not due to a change in values so much as the demand for labour. With relation to Kingston it has been suggested that black girls no longer regard employment in a bank as carrying any prestige, that in fact there are other occupations – government service, teaching, stenography – which are more highly favoured. In other words economic expansion has created a demand for black labour. Another component in the situation is the fact that many black girls now that banks will accept them refuse to take employment with them because of their former attitude.

With the growth of trade and commerce 'new' professions have appeared which have a definite appeal to black people. Two of the most outstanding fields are insurance and accountancy. Opportunities for training exist in Jamaica, and the economic return for professional work of this kind is considerable. Despite this apparently free situation, free that is as regards colour, it is true to say that in almost any type of employment in contemporary Jamaica the possession of a fair skin enhances the opportunities of advancement. In the past 'bad' colour prohibited entry to certain forms of employment, today it merely inhibits progress. There is now a greater demand for qualified people and employers can no longer afford to discriminate on the scale that occurred in the past.

Associated with colour are feelings of assurance and superiority. The near-white individual in Jamaican society socially commands respect from all. In terms of employment this means that he feels capable of handling responsibility, and demonstrates this. On the other hand the black man frequently exhibits to his employer a lack of assurance which provides the perfect rationalization for not advancing him. Granted the historical evolution of the 'white bias' it is not surprising that this should be the case. The fair coloured compensates for his insecurity by an overt assurance; the black man the prey to, perhaps, a more fundamental insecurity, by deference and, at times, a lack of initiative. He is not an African with a reference point beyond and outside the world of the white man, he is a black man in Jamaica with values biased in favour of the white.

Changes of the kind described do not suggest a radical transformation. Modification certainly but little alteration in the basic orientation. Proof of this is to be seen in an analysis of the contemporary social and economic power structure. Twenty years ago it could be said that apart from government power in the island was concentrated in the hands of a relatively small group composed of Jamaica whites, fair coloured, Jews and Lebanese. The same people, or their equivalents, dominate the scene today. The expansion of existing enterprises or the creation of new ones in the fields of commerce and industry is due to the efforts of this group or those associated with them. The fact that there is a black governor-general, or that receptions at King's House are open to all colours is irrelevant to the significance of this continued dominance. The perpetuation of power by this group strengthens the white bias in the society. They are the positive proof to all that power is an attribute of the white or near white. They may be resented but simultaneously they are admired.

One of the fields of endeavour fostered by the fair element is the tourist industry. This has undoubtedly brought prosperity to a limited number of people in the island. The industry reflects some of the changes mentioned above. The hotels of the north coast designed specifically for tourism rely not only on a white American clientele but out of season on the patronage of 'natives'. That they are prohibitively expensive puts them out of bounds for the mass of the population. This type of tourism again provides evidence of the association of power and money with the European. Its parallel might very well be the great house in the days of slavery. There are incidents from time to time of black clients being treated with disrespect by hotel staff themselves black. Such episodes are reported in the press, there are letters to the editor, then all is forgotten.

A quite new institution has appeared on the Jamaican scene in the last two decades – the University. Founded in 1949 as a university college in association with the University of London it achieved full status as a degree-giving body in 1962. For most of the intelligentsia in the British Caribbean political federation was, and is, the only real solution of the problem of nationhood within the area. Inevitably the University was fully behind the federalists throughout the period of the short-lived federation. The young economists, sociologists and historians continue to advocate the federal idea. This has not enamoured them to the government of an independent Jamaica as recent controversies have shown. Although many West Indian students and staff are in favour of Caribbean unity this has not prevented the emergence of real and imagined colour feeling.

At its inception the University in the face of lack of qualified West Indian staff relied very heavily on ex-patriates. As more of the former became available there has been a steady policy of West-indianization. Recruitment has been from all parts of the Caribbean. It is not surprising that coming from backgrounds heavily charged with colour feeling some individuals tend to re-create the sentiments, ideas, and attitudes of those backgrounds in the environment of the University. Clearly none of this is manifested at the overt level. But in the private sector a tendency is observable for those of a particular colour to associate with each other. In this the University merely reflects the wider society.

Public criticism of the University is based very largely on a misconception of what the institution is supposed to be. There is a great deal of respect for its scientific achievements, particularly in the field of medicine. On the other hand the theorizing, as it were, of those in the arts and social sciences is not appreciated. In many people's view the work of the scientist has practical application, that of the social scientist has not. The actual physical setting of the University has not helped to bridge this gap. Many of the staff live on the campus, as do the students, and social contacts with people in Kingston can be minimal. Although misconceptions exist with regard to the University they are not of the magnitude and kind that hamper many of the new universities in Africa. There the gap between the mass of the people and the academic elite is profound, and the institution itself is quite alien. The concept of the mission school inculcating alien European values in a society with a different value system cannot be applied to Jamaica. The model from primary school to university has always been firmly that of Britain.

For the North American and British tourist social life as it is lived in hotels, night-clubs, and diplomatic receptions must appear a perfection of racial harmony. There is today a complete public mixing of all racial groups. This can be misleading and has led even such an experienced observer of the social scene as Peter Abrahams to remark: '. . . there is a striking sense of freedom from colour consciousness. . . . In government offices black and brown and white and yellow work side by side without any reference to colour. . . .'(2) This public manifestation is undoubtedly impressive, particularly to someone from a race-haunted society such as South Africa, but it is a manifestation which still remains very largely a public occurrence.

In the private sector where considerations of employment, business and politics do not necessarily apply the picture is somewhat different. Here again there have been modifications. Marriage, which is the focus of relationships far beyond those of the union of a couple, is still an indicator of the strength of the 'white bias' in the society. Kingston has a preponderance of lighter girls who come from all over the island in search of the jobs and amenities the city has to offer. It is from the ranks of such girls that the up and coming black professional man will tend to choose his future wife. The black educated girl still has to face the problem her predecessor of twenty years ago faced – that her male counterpart prefers a girl lighter than himself as his mate. Her economic opportunities may be greater but her marital choice is as limited as ever. It is obvious that this induces a considerable degree of frustration and discontent.

Amongst middle class brown or fair coloured people the same

marital patterns are perpetuated. A family's choice for a daughter's husband will nearly always be in favour of the fairer man as against the darker man irrespective of the qualifications possessed by either. There are of course exceptions to this pattern of choice but basically the equation of the black or dark with undesirable social and educational characteristics within this group is as strong as it ever was. The outstanding black individual is much more likely to have a European wife than a near-white Jamaican wife. The latter trend began to develop soon after the war when ex-servicemen returned to Jamaica with such wives. The same pattern is exhibited in several West African societies where the motivations within the elite for it are to be seen both in terms of the lack of education amongst African women and in terms of colour.

The fact that such marriages take place is indicative on the one hand of the presence of the 'white bias' but also on the other hand of the tendency to overcome the rigid colour endogamy of the past. If racial friction between European and non-European in the world is to diminish there is no surer way to set about it than by unions of this kind. Unfortunately some authorities appear to be still influenced by a kind of race fear. Margery Perham is a notable example. In her Reith Lectures of 1961 she stated that: 'The Germanic-speaking Europeans – the British, the Americans, the Dutch – share a deep bias against inter-marriage with the Negro race. It is no good our trying to avoid this granite-hard fact. It lies at the very heart of our present problem in Africa. This conscious, or sometimes subconscious, fear of race-mixture accounts both for the white man's innermost ring of defence and also for all his outer ring of political, social and economic ramparts. . . .'(3) If Miss Perham is correct in her view then the whole contemporary chiaroscuro of West Indian colour relationships could never have come into being. It is necessary to examine her thesis somewhat more closely because it is one which not only has a bearing on the perpetuation of the 'white bias' in Jamaica, but is also used, in much cruder forms, as part of a general racialist argument in the world at large.

One of the most intriguing problems still awaiting examination in this field is the variation in attitude and behaviour of particular colonial powers regarding sexual relations, and colour prejudice and discrimination. The Dutch are a case in point. In the early period of Dutch settlement at the Cape in South Africa in the seventeenth century it has been emphasized that: ' . . . with regard to the relations between Europeans and non-Europeans, there appears to be ample evidence that the factors of race and skin-colour as such played little part in determining the attitude of the former to the latter . . . we find that baptism not only conferred upon the individual a legal status but a social status as well, which, in the case of women of full colour, frequently led to marriage with European men. . . .'(4) There has been a long and tortuous development since these almost halcyon days of race relations in South Africa to the contemporary *apartheid* policies and racial legislation. The fact that legislation is necessary in South Africa to prohibit not only marriage but sexual relations between European and non-European is a refutation of the argument that there is a deep European bias against such relations. If the repulsion were so profound as Miss Perham thinks then surely legislation would not be necessary? In this connexion it is interesting to note that white South African women, whether of English or Boer origin, when visiting Europe will often seek out black African men as their sexual partners. A similar predisposition is noticeable among American tourists in Jamaica.

In the case of the United States the vehemence and horror which are expressed by many Americans at the notion of inter-ethnic sex relations can be very misleading. Despite the legislation of individual states against racial intermarriage and repressive social attitudes miscegenation has always existed. For the white American male the historical sexual accessibility of Negro slave women, the influence of Calvinism, and the pattern of white dominance have combined to make the contemporary coloured woman an object of extreme sexual attraction.(5)

Miss Perham's thesis really has to be stood on its head. Fear of race-mixture is not the cause of the European's political and economic domination of the non-European in the past. It is artificially engendered in order to rationalize that domination. Clearly if a people are regarded as sexually repulsive and culturally inadequate they must in fact be inferior. This inferiority confers the right upon the European of creating barriers of discrimination and prejudice in order to keep himself from contamination. The reality of the situation is that despite such barriers racial-mixture has occurred wherever the European has been in contact with the non-European. It is perhaps not an exaggeration to suggest that legal and social barriers against miscegenation have the effect of intensifying it.

The irrelevance of colour itself as a barrier to marriage is demonstrated by the fact that a middle class European woman would have more chances of contracting a happy marriage with an educated, black, middle class Jamaican than with a Croat peasant, or even a working class male from her own society. All the evidence suggests that in the period of initial contact before the process of colonization has begun the sentiments expressed by the European are more concerned with wonderment and excitement rather than repulsion.(6)

That Jamaican society is still predominantly activated by European values in terms of colour, thought, sentiment and behaviour is seen in the failure of any political party or group to achieve success with a platform of a Negro or African Jamaica. It is important in this connexion to recollect that according to the Census of 1960 76 per cent of Jamaicans are classified as African. Two movements with a black or African ethos merit attention.

The beginnings of the Ras Tafari Brethren appear to have been in the 1930's. From its inception there has been an association with Ethiopia and the Emperor Haile Selassie. The latter is regarded as a divinity by the Rastafarians.(7) Although there are a number of factions and groups within the movement the overriding philosophy and policy is concerned with a return to Africa, and specifically to Ethiopia. For the Rastafarians, Haile Selassie's kingdom is their spiritual home and should become their physical home. The attitude of most Jamaicans of all colours towards the Rastafarians is one of derision and good-natured toleration. They inhabit that part of the Kingston slums known as the Dungle or dung-hill. Many have had a reasonable education and are addicted to philosophical ramblings in which the ills of the world, of Jamaica, the benefits of Africa and the ideology of the old Testament are inextricably mixed up.

Set apart from the majority of the population by their clothing and length of hair, and in the case of some a liking for ganga, the Rastafarians appear to be absolutely sincere in their affection for Africa and their desire to return there. In this they are the legitimate successors to Marcus Garvey and his Back to Africa Movement. Violence has never been an attribute of the Rastafarians. The sole exception was the faction which supported the egregious Claudius Henry and his son in 1959. Their attempts to take over the government in Jamaica resulted in the death of three Rastafarians and two British soldiers. This minor outbreak attracted a great deal of attention in Jamaica and people began to think of the Brethren as a violent, subversive group. Fortunately the University had been approached by a number of Rastafarian leaders for educational assistance, and assistance against current victimization. The response of the University was to send a team of experts to investigate and report on Rastafarianism. Its findings were published in 1960.(8)

Perhaps the most interesting conclusion reached by the research team is that contained in the following quotation:

'For Jamaican leftists, the violent part of the Rastafarian spectrum is a gift. Capitalist, bourgeois and proletariat can be directly translated into white, brown and black. Revolution becomes Redemption with Repatriation as the issue provoking bloodshed. . . . In so far as this political philosophy employs the ideology of Rastafarian racism, its spread through the bulk of the population is assured, unless Government takes positive steps to meet the legitimate needs of the lower classes, including the Rastafarian group. The choice before Jamaica is that between social reform which is planned, peaceful and rapid on the one hand, or changes of a different sort. It is certain that Jamaican society cannot continue in its present form, since economic development presumes social stability, this means that any successful development depends on an intelligent programme of social reform. The recent spread of Rastafarian doctrine among educated middle class youths is largely due to the appeals of ganga and Marxism, but this spread will surely continue as long as Jamaican society fails to provide the young with significant ideals of social justice for which to strive and opportunities for their achievement . . .'(9)

The action taken by the Government, that of Mr Manley and the People's National Party, was to send a mission, comprised of Rastafarians and others, to Africa to investigate the possibilities of repatriation. It is interesting to speculate if the same response would have been forthcoming from the present, Jamaica Labour Party, Government. The mission issued its report in 1961. Its recommendations were as obvious as might be expected – that African countries need skilled personnel at all levels and would welcome Jamaicans in a number of categories. So far as we are aware there has been no active emigration to Ethiopia or elsewhere in Africa on the part of Jamaicans. Whatever plans the P.N.P. government may have had to implement such emigration were halted by the imminence of the general election in 1962 in which Bustamante was successful. Since that time the Jamaican Labour Party has evinced no interest whatsoever in repatriation to Africa.

In the seven years since the University published its report on

Rastafarianism there has been no striking evidence that Rastafarianism has increased its hold on the population. Primarily it is a movement of protest against abominable living conditions, and lack of economic and social opportunity on the part of the black, dispossessed slum dwellers of Kingston. What has lent them a spur is the constant spectacle of the improving conditions of the brown middle classes in the city. What has hindered the spread of the movement is precisely its identification with things African.

A somewhat different movement from Rastafarianism was Millard Johnson's black man's party, the People's Progressive Party. It could be regarded as the lineal descendant of Garvey's People's Political Party. Unlike Garvey, however, Millard Johnson is not interested in the repatriation of Jamaicans to Africa – he wishes Jamaica to become more African. Founded a year before the elections of 1962, the People's Progressive Party went down to massive defeat at the polls – it received 12,616 votes out of a total of over half a million cast. It is possible that a nine-month period in which to organize an island-wide political apparatus is too short, and that given more time and a better organization Millard Johnson would command a degree of success. On the other hand it is much more likely that even in the best circumstances there would be no mass support for a black Jamaica programme. Millard Johnson, a middle class black Jamaican, does not possess the dynamic fervour of a Garvey or a Bustamante.

Although because of the persistence of the 'white bias' an appeal to the black electorate to support the ideal of a black or African Jamaica would be of dubious success it is possible that economic difficulties might produce a radical change. If the economic opportunity for the mass of black Jamaicans remains as limited as it is at present, and prosperity continues to shine on the middle and upper class coloured groups, then a black leadership may emerge which will capture the imagination of the masses. If neither the P.N.P. nor the Jamaica Labour Party can produce a solution for the dispossessed condition of the black Jamaican proletariat within the next ten years revolutionary changes would seem inevitable.

Discussion of changes in the class and colour relationships in the last two decades leads inevitably to a consideration of the problems connected with the Jamaican search for identity. This search is of a different kind from that of the newly emergent nations of Africa. The difference lies in the fact that although both the Caribbean and Africa have been profoundly influenced by Europe Africa possesses indigenous cultures which at the present time are undergoing a vigorous reappraisal. With few exceptions the African as a slave in the West Indies was systematically deprived of his cultural heritage. In Jamaica some folkloric elements persist but it would be true to say that despite the occasional resort to Obeah and the telling of Anansi stories, the Jamaican peasant is at an immense cultural remove from his African counterpart. Polygyny, ancestor worship, and fetishism are prominent features of the socio-cultural complex of West African societies. They are meaningless in the Jamaican context. Plantation slavery was the matrix from which the Jamaican peasant evolved. In many ways his experience was similar to that of the Negro in the United States, who is primarily a product of American culture.

The European in the West Indies was a colonist in the proper sense – he came to stay. In West Africa his role was that of the transient – the mosquito-inhibited settlement. Wherever there has been permanent European settlement the environment has dictated very largely the evolution of the culture. The way of life of the farmer in the Australian outback represents a profound modification of the culture from which he came.

The Creole culture of Jamaica is not an amalgam of European and African strains. It is a synthesis of the culture of the plantation and that of Europe. Both the Negro and the planter were profoundly influenced by the structure of society which the latter had created in the tropics. Gilberto Freyre has documented this process brillantly in the case of Brazil.(10) That the process was one in which both elements influenced each other is indicated in this quotation from *Lady Nugent's Journal.*

'Many of the ladies, who have not been educated in England, speak a sort of broken English, with an indolent drawing out of the words, that is very tiresome if not disgusting. I stood next to a lady one night, near a window, and, by way of saying something, remarked that the air was much cooler than usual; to which she answered, "*Yes, ma-am, him rail-ly too fra-ish.*"'(11) Today the English spoken by all educated Jamaicans irrespective of colour is quite distinct in terms of pronunciation, accent, inflexion, tone and vocabulary from standard English – as distinct as that of Australian English. Peasant dialect in Jamaica is a complex of African words, the English of seventeenth century white indentured servants, and standard English.(12)

It was not only, however, a question of speech for the Negro slave influenced the behaviour of the social superiors he himself imitated. An eighteenth century observer, Henry Long, comments on this.

Describing life on the plantation he writes: 'We may see, in some of these places, a very fine young woman, awkwardly dangling her arms with the air of a Negroe-servant, lolling almost the whole day upon beds or settees, her head muffled up with two or three handkerchiefs, her dress loose and without stays. At noon, we find her employed in gobbling pepper-pot seated on the floor, with her sable hand-maids around her. In the afternoon, she takes her *siesto* as usual; while two of these damsels refresh her face with the gentle breathings of the fan; and a third provokes the drowsy powers of Morpheus by delicious scratchings on the sole of either foot. . . . Her ideas are narrowed to the ordinary subjects that pass before her, the business of the plantation, the tittle-tattle of the parish, the tricks, superstitions, diversions and profligate discourses, of the black servants, equally illiterate and unpolished . . .'(13)

This paucity of intellectual interest and indolence is not entirely unknown in the Jamaican upper classes today – the energy may be found for bridge and charitable fund raising, but little else.

In contemporary Jamaica the gap between the black peasant on the one side and the near-white and white upper classes on the other may appear to be profound but close observation demonstrates that they may have more in common with each other than the upper classes have with their English counterparts. For example the Victorian abandon with which these classes created bastards is matched by the disregard for marital institutions which is so characteristic of the peasant. My thesis here is that despite the proliferation of colour distinctions all groups in Jamaica have their cultural roots in each other. This interaction and interdependence is the greatest barrier in the way of the recognition of things African.

The young black intellectual in Jamaica because of the dead hand of the 'white bias' may feel a nostalgic, romantic attachment for the idea of Africa. He may even visit Africa in one capacity or another, and be enthralled. This, however, is a very different matter from real identification with African culture which in essence is wholly alien to the Caribbean. The behaviour of West Indian colonies, as it were, in West Africa further emphasizes this point. They tend to mix almost exclusively with westernized Africans and have little or no contact with true African culture. Black Jamaican missionaries may have gone to Africa as early as 1846 but that continent for the vast majority of Jamaicans has remained almost entirely unknown.

The impress of the plantation and of Europe is indelible. The search for identity must be prepared to accept this. The 'white bias' must be used to advantage, not as a weapon for petty distinctions which degrade and destroy the individual. The cultural inheritance from Europe is vast. Transmuted and transformed by the tropical environment it can become the vehicle of expression for that which is essentially Jamaican. Ethnic origin in terms of Jamaica is a vast irrelevancy.

NOTES AND REFERENCES

1. The office of *custos* of a Jamaican parish is analogous to that of a lord lieutenant of an English county.
2. Peter Abrahams, *Jamaica*, London, 1947, p. 128.
3. Margery Perham, *The Colonial Reckoning*, The Reith Lectures: 1961. Revised and expanded, London, 1963, p. 64.
4. I. D. MacCrone, *Race Attitudes in South Africa*, London, 1937, pp. 40–1, 42.
5. For a discussion of the theme, see Calvin C. Hernton, *Sex and Racism in America*, N.Y., 1965, Chapter IV.
6. The process of change in attitude with relation to the Hottentot is traced in Janheinz Jahn, *Wir Nannten Sie Wilde*, Munich, 1964.
7. The history and ideology of the movement is discussed in M. G. Smith, R. Augier and R. Nettleford, *The Ras Tafari Movement in Kingston, Jamaica*, Jamaica, 1960.
8. Ibid.
9. Ibid., pp. 25, 28.
10. Gilberto Freyre, *The Masters and the Slaves*, and *The Mansions and the Shanties*, London, 1966.
11. *Lady Nugent's Journal*, ed. Frank Cundall, London, 1907, p. 132.
12. See Frederic G. Cassidy, *Jamaica Talk*, London, 1961, p. 21.
13. Edward Long, *History of Jamaica*, London, 1774, p. 52.

APPENDIX I

Land Tenure

THE land tenure system in Jamaica is discussed at some length in Lord Olivier's *Jamaica*, London, 1936, pp. 269–90. See also T. S. Simey, *Welfare and Planning in the West Indies*, Oxford, 1946, pp. 167–73; Report of the Agricultural Policy of Committee of Jamaica, Kingston, 1945; A. J. Wakefield, *Agricultural Development in Jamaica*, London, 1942; Report of the Lands Department, Jamaica, 1945; and Report of Tenancy Reform Committee, Kingston, 1942.

'The rural population of Jamaica comprises approximately 1,013,000 persons. Of these 362,199 reported that they were resident on farms. The remainder of the rural population consisted of persons living on small plots of land other than farms, and those living in villages in semi-rural conditions; 137,095 of the farm population were under 14 years of age, and 225,104 were 14 years of age and over.' (Jamaica Census 1943.)

The writer is indebted to H. Maynair, Esq., of Kingston, Jamaica, for the information contained in the following note.

The uncertainty of ownership of property in rural districts is clearly illustrated by the following analysis of the nature of the titles held by 808 occupiers taken at random from the summary of damage by earthquake in the parish of St Elizabeth in 1943.

TABLE 1

Nature of title held	*No.*	*Percentage of total*
Receipt of diagram	13	1·6
Receipt only	399	49·3
No title	122	15·1
'Gift'	81	10·0
'Inheritance'	28	3·4
Valid title	74	9·2
Will	16	2·0
Diagram only	15	2·0
Tax receipts	25	3·1
'Documents'	25	3·1
Family land	10	1·2

TABLE 2

Jamaica total acreage	Size of farm in acres													
	Total No. of holdings	Total farms	1 to under 2	2 to under 3	3 to under 4	4 to under 6	6 to under 10	10 to under 25	25 to under 50	50 to under 100	100 to under 200	200 to under 500	500 to under 1,000	1,000 and over
	100	100	100	100	100	100	100	100	100	100	100	100	100	100
1. Holding	16·4	34·2	55·9	41·7	36·9	33·5	25·0	23·2	22·7	29·8	34·4	49·6	61·3	40·0
2. "	36·7	38·3	36·5	44·2	42·5	40·1	39·9	33·1	27·1	25·4	29·2	23·1	22·7	30·3
3. "	25·8	17·9	6·7	11·9	16·4	19·1	23·7	24·7	22·3	17·1	15·7	11·5	6·8	15·6
4. "	11·9	6·2	·7	1·9	3·5	5·5	8·2	11·9	14·0	11·9	7·1	6·6	1·9	5·7
5. "	5·0	2·1	·2	·2	·6	1·5	2·2	4·4	7·1	7·6	5·8	5·0	3·4	3·9
6. "	2·1	·7	*	·1	·1	·2	·7	1·7	3·4	3·5	4·0	1·0	1·9	1·2
7. "	·9	·3	—	—	—	·1	·2	·5	1·7	1·3	1·8	1·3	·5	·3
8. "	·5	·1	—	—	—	*	·1	·3	·7	1·4	·2	1·1	·5	·6
9. "	·3	·1	—	—	—	*	·0	·1	·5	·8	1·0	·5	—	1·2
10. "	·4	·1	—	—	—	·0	—	·1	·5	1·2	·8	·3	1·0	1·0

* denotes a very small percentage.

TABLE 3

Jamaica													
	All farms	1 to under 2 acres	2 to under 3 acres	3 to under 4 acres	4 to under 6 acres	6 to under 10 acres	10 to under 25 acres	25 to under 50 acres	50 to under 100 acres	100 to under 200 acres	200 to under 500 acres	500 to under 1,000 acres	10,00 acres and over
Total acreage	100	100	100	100	100	100	100	100	100	100	100	100	100
Acres owned	59·7	57·3	64·7	72·6	78·6	85·2	88·8	88·3	85·5	77·5	71·1	50·0	44·1
Acres rented	6·4	42·6	34·4	27·4	21·4	14·7	11·0	9·3	8·4	5·5	3·3	3·4	2·6
Acres managed	33·9	·1	·9	*	·0	·1	·2	2·4	6·1	17·0	25·6	46·6	53·3

* denotes a very small percentage.

In Jamaica to establish a valid title to land it is necessary to comply with the Land Registration Law which demands the furnishing of a diagram, receipt of a bill of sale, etc. Table 1 illustrates the uncertainty of tenure. The writer was able to corroborate this data from observations in the field and evidence from government surveyors who when surveying road improvement schemes were constantly asking people to show proof that they owned their land and meeting with their inability to do so.

Table 2, taken from the 1943 Census, shows the percentage distribution of farms according to number of holdings and size of farms. It is to be noted that quite a high percentage, 36·7 per cent, have two holdings which illustrates the dual ownership mentioned in the text.

Table 3 shows the percentage distribution of farms by acres owned, rented, and managed in Jamaica. A definite majority of farmland is 'owned' as against rented or managed; as acreage increases, in the case of individual farms the proportion of those rented drops.

A number of different types of tenure was provided for in the tabulation of the Census, and the numbers of farm operators falling within different categories are as follows:

TABLE 4

Owners	38,270
Owners and cash tenants	16,899
Owners and kind tenants	1,342
Owners and work performed tenants	675
Owners and shared cash tenants	527
Owners and improved land tenants	992
Cash tenants	4,802
Kind tenants	1,010
Work performed tenants	353
Share and cash tenants	342
Improved land tenants	368
Managers	593
Total	66,173

Table 5 gives the percentage of farmers who worked off the farms together with the average number of weeks worked off the farm in 1942. Over a third of farmers worked off their farms which seems to show that farming in Jamaica is not sufficient in itself to support the individual farmers.

Table 6 shows the percentage of those farmers who worked away from their farms who were engaged on farm labour and general labour. It is seen that nearly a third, 31·9 per cent, were engaged in farm labour.

TABLE 5

	Jamaica												
	Size of farm												
	1 to under 2 acres	2 to under 3 acres	3 to under 4 acres	4 to under 6 acres	6 to under 10 acres	10 to under 25 acres	25 to under 50 acres	50 to under 100 acres	100 to under 200 acres	200 to under 500 acres	500 to under 1,000 acres	1,000 acres and over	All farms
Per cent of operators who worked away from farm	48·6	40·6	37·5	33·1	29·0	23·5	19·9	22·3	19·3	21·0	11·6	12·0	33·1
Average number of weeks worked away from farm (all operators)	8·9	6·8	6·3	5·4	4·8	4·4	4·4	5·9	5·9	6·7	3·3	2·5	5·8
Average number of weeks worked away from farm (operators who worked off farms)	18·3	16·8	16·7	16·3	16·4	18·6	22·0	26·6	30·4	31·8	28·4	2·1	17·5

TABLE 6

	All farms No.	Per cent	1 to under 2 acres	2 to under 3 acres	3 to under 4 acres	4 to under 6 acres	6 to under 10 acres	10 to under 25 acres	25 to under 50 acres	50 to under 100 acres	100 to under 200 acres	200 to under 500 acres	500 to under 1,000 acres	1,000 acres and over
All farmers	66,173													
Farmers with other occupations	21,927	100	100	100	100	100	100	100	100	100	100	100	100	100
Farm labourer	6,989	31·9	48·8	41·6	35·2	30·0	22·3	13·7	8·6	6·7	4·2	2·5	4·2	—
General labourer	4,897	22·3	20·6	23·3	25·3	25·3	23·6	19·1	12·4	10·0	4·2	1·3	—	—

TABLE 7

Years on present farm	All farms	1 to under 2	2 to under 3	3 to under 4	4 to under 6	6 to under 10	10 to under 25	25 to under 50	50 to under 100	100 to under 200	200 to under 500	500 to under 1,000	1,000 and over
All farmers	100	100	100	100	100	100	100	100	100	100	100	100	100
Resident for under 1 year	·5	·4	·4	·3	·5	·4	·5	·8	1·8	2·2	4·5	5·3	4·5
1 year	2·7	6·2	2·8	2·1	2·1	2·0	1·7	2·0	1·9	4·4	4·2	9·2	6·3
2 years	5·4	8·8	7·0	6·3	5·2	4·1	3·5	2·6	2·9	5·6	7·1	10·2	5·2
3 years	6·1	9·0	7·2	7·1	6·4	4·9	4·2	3·2	3·1	6·0	5·5	4·8	6·6
4 years	4·8	7·2	6·1	5·5	5·1	3·8	3·1	2·3	3·7	3·6	3·6	3·9	4·5
5–9 years	18·5	22·8	23·3	20·7	19·2	16·9	13·2	12·3	13·8	14·1	16·3	16·4	13·8
10–14 years	17·1	16·7	18·4	18·8	17·6	17·6	16·0	13·1	11·5	13·3	14·4	16·4	15·3
15–19 years	9·7	7·8	8·8	9·7	10·1	10·3	10·6	10·1	10·6	8·1	12·1	10·6	10·5
20–24 years	12·1	8·3	9·7	10·7	12·2	13·6	15·0	15·3	12·0	14·3	13·9	8·7	13·8
25 years and over	23·1	12·8	16·3	18·8	21·6	26·4	32·2	38·3	38·7	28·4	18·4	14·5	19·5

TABLE 8

Size of farm in acres	Racial origin of farmers								
	All races	Coloured	Black	White N.O.S.	British Isles	European	Chinese	East Indian	Others
All farms	100	18·8	78·2	·7	·6	·2	·1	1·4	*
1 to under 2	100	13·0	84·9	·2	·1	*	·1	1·7	*
2 " 3	100	14·4	83·5	·2	·2	·1	·1	1·5	*
3 " 4	100	14·8	83·6	·2	·1	·1	·1	1·1	*
4 " 6	100	16·3	81·9	·2	·1	·1	·1	1·3	*
6 " 10	100	18·0	79·7	·4	·2	·2	·1	1·3	·1
10 " 25	100	23·6	73·4	·7	·5	·2	·1	1·5	*
25 " 50	100	32·9	62·0	1·5	1·1	·4	·3	1·6	·2
50 " 100	100	42·3	48·3	3·2	2·5	·7	·4	2·1	·5
100 " 200	100	44·7	38·8	7·1	6·0	1·2	·2	1·6	·4
200 " 500	100	44·6	26·0	12·3	12·1	1·0	·3	2·4	1·3
500 " 1,000	100	42·5	18·4	20·3	15·0	1·9	—	—	1·9
1,000 and over	100	37·6	10·8	21·0	28·2	·6	·3	·9	·6

* N.O.S. denotes not otherwise specified.

Table 7 illustrates the change-over in ownership or tenure of farmers in Jamaica. In the case of farms of 100 acres and over there is a considerably larger number of change-overs than is the case with those below 100 acres.

Table 8 gives the percentage distribution of farms according to racial origin and size of farm. When it is remembered that the white groups are only 1·1 per cent of the population it will be seen that they control nearly 50 per cent of the farms over 1,000 acres, that is to say 50 per cent of the large estates and properties in Jamaica are owned by Europeans, or by American interests. This shows the strong economic background of the 'white bias' in the society. Black people possess a majority of all farms, 78·2 per cent, as well as a majority of those from 1 to under 2 acres, 84·9 per cent. The black people constituting 78·1 per cent of the population owns only 10·8 per cent of farms of 1,000 acres and over.

APPENDIX II

A Schoolgirl's Diary

THIS extract from a schoolgirl's diary gives a picture of life in Jamaica from the point of view of an adolescent girl of the lower class. The writer was fourteen years old at the time of the diary and still attending elementary school. She lived with her 'aunty'. Her mother was alive but her father had died some time ago. Punctuation and language have been left as in the original.

DIARY

Wednesday I got up at six o'clock tidy up one room. I shine three pairs of shoes. Comb my hair my self. I went to the Bakery to buy Bread. I had my bath at seven o'clock under a shower in a zinc round bathroom but it had a top. My Aunt prepared breakfast for my Step Uncle and seven others. I had for breakfast bread an butter an a can of choclate tea and some corn meal porrige. I went to school a little later at half past nine. Two health Nurses came to school. My heart beat heard for I was a little afraid. She came to give us injection [against typhoid]. I got my own, at first a moneta for the school came and rub my left hand with a bit of cotton and some lotion on it. The nurse took the needle and fill it with medicine she sent it right up in my arm but I did not cry, then another moneta rub my arm a second time. I went home for dinner at 12 o'clock. I got one cassava flour dumplin a piece of yellow yam pumpkin sweet potatoes and a piece of beef and I came back to school, but all this time my hand was paining me, but I continued my school work. About half past three I went to drawing class I draw a flower pot. At four o'clock I was back home. When I came home I went to cottage to a lady. I spend a long time up there playing with the children. When I went home my aunt quarrelled with me and she hit me over my back and said 'This will learn you that when I send you out again you must not stay long.' She gave me a sixpence to buy bread for supper I got for my supper Bread and butter and fry plaintain and a can of corn porrige. I wash up all the supper thing and caught up a fowl with eight chickens. I went to bed at nine o'clock.
Thursday I got up at halfpast five, clean out the drawing room and dust down the chairs. I tidy out one bedroom. I sat down reading a piece of old

paper an my aunt said to me 'what the hell you doing with the piece of old paper an you have a lot of things to do before you go to school.' I clean three pairs of shoes, comb my hair, an catch up the fire at six o'clock. I went an buy penny half penny worth of chocolate for the tea. My aunt told me to leave the fireside an she will complet the breakfast. I bought a six pence worth of bread for the breakfast. I had my bath and dress myself for school. At half past eight she send me up to Red Hazel for some grape fruits. I made my return very quick for I was feeling hungry I got for my breakfast a can of chocolate an bread an butter an a Johnny cake. When I look on the clock it was five minutes to nine she said 'that I must go to the sea side and buy fish.' I told her I could not go because I was late. She said to me you bitch you you see what you eat 12 o'clock for your dinner. I said 'I dont care'. As she was going to knock me I ran out of the house and go to school. I went to school quarter past nine. Thursday morning is always scripture so I read my bible. We had grammar an arithmetic test. At 12 o'clock I went home for my dinner. my aunt did not say anything about what I told her this morning. I got for my dinner plain rice, yellow yam, potatoes and fish. I went back to school at 1 o'clock. When I was leaving the house I hear my aunt and her husband having a little quarrelled it was about. When the dinner ready he wont come home befor the dinner cold. Hear him what the hell you worrying me for my good woman. I went home from school ten to five. When I went home she was sleeping. I took my own time and undress my self an catch up the fire. I cooked the supper we had for supper fry fish, Johnny cake and bread and tea. I wash up my supper things an catch up my chickens when I went in side my aunt said to me you bitch you and flogged me and send me to bed. I went to bed half past eight. I dont even tell anyone goodnight.

Friday I got up at 7 o'clock. I did not clean any shoe, I comb my hair and go to the bakery. I did not bath, because the pipe was, lock off. They were working on the pipe. All the same I use water. I got for my breakfast bread an butter and a can of mint tea. I went to school at half past eight. I began to do my hand work, because Friday morning is our handwork day. I have completed on mat. I went home for my dinner at 12 o'clock I did not get plenty dinner so I was vexed I only got a piece of yellow some rice and cod fish an a piece of pear. My aunt saw that I was vexed so she said to me, 'you bitch you, you provided any thing Hear you just come out of the house an leave me in peace. I took my hat an came to school. When I came back I took my composition Book and transcribe my work in a new book. I try to be neat as possible. I went home at half past four. When I came home from school I carried some milk up to a lady. When I came back I went to the bakery for bread, for supper. When I came back I began to peel a roast breadfruit the breadfruit drop from me and a big piece break off. I aet it I said to myself that is to make up for my dinner. When I went inside with it my aunt said to me 'Eileen! is the whole of the breadfruit that,' I said 'Yes mam'. She said 'you bitch you, you never get a piece of it tonight for you eat your share already.' I got for my supper bread an tea. I did not take up the chicken the way I was vexed. I got one flogging, that I will never forget I went to my bed at eight o'clock feeling very sad.

Saturday I got up at five, prepare breakfast for My Aunt Husband's Brother going to Kingston by train. I got for his breakfast some coffee tea an a few slice of bread an butter. I went to the market at six o'clock to get beef. I got 3½ lbs of beef for 3/2½ an a 1lb of pork. I took a 2*d* out of the change an I bought a 1*d* pear and 1*d* break an I ate 1 for I was very hungry I never leave the market until 15 minutes past nine I had my breakfast at half past nine I got bread an butter an a cup of chocolate tea. I work very hard during the day. I got my dinner at twelve o'clock I got beef soup and fish. I began to iron at one o'clock I completed at 5 o'clock. I began to clean at half past five. I had to clean out four apartment. I finish at half past seven.

APPENDIX III

Fragment of a Lower Class Autobiography

THE writer of the following life story is a black lower class woman aged 34 who was brought up in a Christian Family. She is a woman of some character and above average intelligence. The text is unedited.

'I was told by my mother that I was born on a Saturday the 21st day of May, also she named me Edith for my father's mother who was according to her a very good woman. I doubt that I am good, my life story you can best judge for yourself.

'My parents were real humble. God fearing, country folk. They lived all their lives in the district of Nonsuch, just five miles from the town of Port Antonio. To reach this district you have to travel five miles of continuous hill with the houses jotted between. I had two uncles and an aunt, my mother's two brothers and a sister, also my grandparents, two older sisters and my aunt's seven children. We all lived on a hill overlooking the school, which served as a mission for the keeping of Sunday School and religious services, whenever the minister from Port Antonio could come there.

'My grandfather was an easy going man, we children could always get away with anything when he is around, but not so with our grandmother. She was a very stern woman and would always remind us of hell fire. Their home was a large one and every Saturday night the whole family sleeps there to be at hand to take part in Sunday morning devotions. Those Saturday nights used to be special nights for us children because of the 'Bread Basket' that was always opened to give us a taste of the Sunday bread ere we go to bed. On Sundays mornings we were always awakened at five o'clock to get on our knees for the break-of-day-prayer. When I say on your knees I mean stay there for an hour or more while two or three of the older people pray to their hearts content and then sing a hymn before you could be allowed to get off your knees.

'After the singing of this hymn the older people go around *saying* good morning, in the meantime warning us children that "*today is the Sabbath* you must speak quietly and don't play about for the Loar wont love you for you will surely get a flogging on Monday. I can't help remarking about my grandmother, she was a sly old girl and all we children were afraid of her. If we did a wrong she acted as if she never noticed it, days will pass when you kind of feel secure, then suddenly she would ask you to fetch her a fine stick to light her pipe, and giving her the stick she would suddenly hold on to your hand and give you a good flogging. I called her an old brute one day and promised her a flogging whenever I became a woman, but I am glad to say I never carry out that threat. When I was just a little tot my mother call me to her one day and she showed me certain places on my body that she said belong to my father and that I should not alloy any boys or men to touch. My father was very good and kind to us and knowing. I have something that belongs to him.

'I never allowed a boy to come within a yard of me during my childhood days. I was a little satan at home. So it was a relief to my parents the time came for me to go to school I remember the morning as it was yesterday. My father wanted to take me and my mother wanted to go also, however, both went with me. I was much spoiled child at home. The teacher knowing about this greeted us thus: – Well, well so it take you both to bring Emily to school, "she wont be able to tule me as she is doing with you both." I felt at the time like returning home, also my father told the teacher that if he takes time with me and dont use the bullying method and you will find me quite good and willing.

'I was call "sister" at home, but teacher he calls me Edith but I did not like and I would not answer to that name at first, so we had a lot of fudd for the first few weeks. To make matters worse I had a bad lapse in my speech, and could not call certain words properly viz: sugar, bottle, candle, etc., this create a lot of teasing from the older children and fights I wage until I sometime reach home half nude. Going home like this always hurt my mother, but my father laugh it off and say "Sis you are learning to defend yourself, haven't a brother to fight for you, you will always have to do it for yourself, but do not bite and scratch anyone as not to leave any scar on them." Hearing this from my father was enough so I fought my way through school, boy or girl made no difference to me. My teacher could just look at me and know when I am contemplating to fight someone. He used to keep me in school in some pretence of doing some extra work until the other children are out of my reach on their way home. It was during one of these fights that I got the greatest shock of my childhood life. This made me stop and think and grew up overnight.

'A girl that I was fighting with told me in a fit of temper that my father is not my father or in other words the person who I took for my father was only my mother's husband. I believe at the time she was telling an untruth and I try to get at her tongue but teacher came between us and took her away. He told me it wasn't true and I should not notice it but the way he said it to me was not convincing. When she saw me coming home she thought I was sick and came to enquire what was wrong, I could not keep from balling out for quite a while before I told her what was the matter, she told me what I had heard was quite true and that she wanted to tell me a long time but my step father advise her not to do so. He had not a child of his own and wanted me to believe I was his. I then asked about my two elder sisters and she told me that they had known long before but that it made no difference to them, so it shouldn't do so to me. I asked as was expected, about my own father, only to find out that he already had a wife and four children when he made this association with our mother. Then it was that I understood the meaning of the vast predictions that my grandmother made concerning me. I then and there promised never to bring an illegitimate child into the world and by Gods will I have kept that promise. It was a sad face which my step-father (for that is what I now called him), saw when he came home from his work that evening. As usual he called me to come and have some of his dinner with him, I went but could swallow never a bite, I just sat there and cried my eyes swollen. Surprised he asked what was wrong, and having been told the cause he forgot the dinner and accompanied my in crying. My eldest sister Elma started quarrelling she said both she and Bea knew about these happenings quite a long time ago and that it made no difference to them, then why should I be picking up a row and made everyone feel out of place, she said that he was just as much our father as he is our mother's husband. My grandmother who came up to visit us just when this was going on, said my step-father should be glad I was not his child, because I am no credit to anyone – I am just a spoiled, wicked child. I was not surprised hearing this from her, she was always preparing hell and horror for me, so I just gave her a dirty look and slip outside the house. I asked my mother that night to allow me to sleep in bed with she and my step-father, I felt at the time that I just want to be near him. She granted my request, so I slept with them for quite a few weeks, before returning to our own room. I was a bright scholar at school, and used to outshine the others in my class, so my teacher told me that if I continue like that, I will surely become a teacher one day. That remark made me very ambitious, so much so, that I started on it and finally put the idea in to my parents head. Then I was told by my mother that I was born under the Planet "Ares" and people born under this Planet always become teachers this cause me to study even more, with a determination to be above every child in school. I might have reached my goal in becoming a teacher, but fate stepped in when I was not even half way through school. My mother started gettting sick sometimes for as much as four months out of the year. She always started getting sick in August and she kept that way till sometimes in January of the succeeding year. This affect me mostly because my two elder sisters left home when I was quite young, so I have to stay home with my mother, when my step-father is at work in the fields. And then about this time we started having Hurricanes almost every year. From a little tot I was made to realise that our very existence depend on the Bananas that were planted, before the house, behind the house and both sides of the house. My step-father used to hold me up to a window and pointed to a Banana that just shoot out the day before and tell me how many hand that was, and how long it will be ready to "cut". So when these hurricanes came and blew down our bananas, and we stand and look at the trees lying down, it kind of broke down our morale. It used to be very hard fights these days to keep our body clothed and getting something to eat. These hurricanes were kind a spiteful, they always came in the month of August when all the fruit trees are laden. I remember one night during one of these hurricanes – my step-father was taking me off our hill down to the school, the roof of our house had just blown off, on his way going down the "hill" I was blown out of his hand, he started searching for me and I for him till we both found each other a few yards from the school. It was no joke having a sick mother to look after these days. I just couldn't share between school and home, so my schooling was affected through having to stay home with my sick mother.'

Bibliography

Peter Abrahams, *Jamaica*, London, 1957.
Morley Ayearst, *The British West Indies*, London, 1960.
W. Beckford, *A Descriptive Account of Jamaica*, London, 1790.
Martha Beckwith, *Black Roadways*, Chapel Hill, 1929.
W. Bell, *Jamaican Leaders*, California, 1964.
C. V. Black, *The Story of Jamaica*, London, 1965.
Judith Blake, *Family Structure in Jamaica*, N.Y., 1961.
G. W. Bridges, *The Annals of Jamaica*, London, 1827.
Sir Alan Burns, *History of the British West Indies*, London, 1954.
W. L. Burns, *Emancipation and Apprenticeship in the West Indies*, London, 1928.
T. Carlyle, *Letters of Oliver Cromwell*, London, 1870.
F. G. Cassidy, *Jamaica Talk*, London, 1961.
Census of Jamaica 1943, Kingston, 1944.
K. B. Clark, *Prejudice and your Child*, N.Y., 1955.
Edith Clarke, *My Mother Who Fathered Me*, London, 1957.
Y. Cohen, 'Structure and Function in Family Organization and Socialization in a Jamaican Community', *American Anthropologist*, Vol. LVIII, No. 4, 1956.
T. Cooper, *Facts Illustrative of the Condition of the Negro Slaves in Jamaica*, London, 1824.
G. R. Coulthard, *Race and Colour in Caribbean Literature*, Oxford, 1962.
E. D. Cronon, *Black Moses: The Story of Marcus Garvey*, N.Y., 1964.
F. C. Cundall and J. C. Pietersz, *Jamaica Under the Spaniards*, Kingston, 1919.
F. C. Cundall, ed., *Lady Nugent's Journal*, London, 1907.
P. D. Curtin, *The Two Jamaicas*, Cambridge, Mass., 1955.
H. Dallas, *History of the Maroon War*, London, 1790.
A. Davis, B. Gardner and Mary B. Gardner, *Deep South*, Chicago, 1941.
I. De A. Reid, 'The Negro in the British West Indies', *Journal of Negro Education*, Vol. X, No. 3.
J. Dollard, *Caste and Class in a Southern Town*, N.Y., 1957.
Cedric Dover, *Half-Caste*, London, 1937.

Bryan Edwards, *History of the West Indies*, London, 1796.
O. C. Francis, *The People of Modern Jamaica*, Department of Statistics, Jamaica, 1963.
Franklin Frazier, *The Negro Family in the United States*, Chicago, 1939.
Gilberto Freyre, *The Masters and the Slaves*, London, 1946.
— *The Mansions and the Shanties*, London, 1966.
— *The Racial Factor in Contemporary Politics*, Sussex, 1965.
W. J. Gardner, *History of Jamaica*, London, 1909.
A. Jacques Garvey, *Garvey and Garveyism*, Jamaica, 1963.
Elsa Goveia, *A Study on the Historiography of the British West Indies to the End of the Nineteenth Century*, Mexico, 1956.
D. Hall, *Free Jamaica 1838–68*, Yale, 1959.
John Hearne and R. Nettleford, *Our Heritage*, Extra-Mural Studies Department, U.W.I., Jamaica, 1963.
Fernando Henriques, 'Colour Values in Jamaican Society', *British Journal of Sociology*, Vol. II, No. 2, 1951.
— 'Kinship and Death in Jamaica', *Phylon*, Vol. XIII, No. 3, 1951.
— *Jamaica*, London, 1957.
— 'West Indian Family Organization', *American Journal of Sociology*, Vol. IV, No. 1, 1949.
C. C. Hernton, *Sex and Racism in America*, N.Y., 1965.
M. J. Herskovits, *The Myth of the Negro Past*, N.Y., 1941.
— *Trinidad Village*, N.Y., 1947.
— *Life in a Haitian Valley*, N.Y., 1937.
— *Rebel Destiny*, N.Y., 1934.
Janheinz Jahn, *Wir Nannten Sie Wilde*, Munich, 1964.
H. H. Johnston, *The Negro in the New World*, London, 1913.
Madeleine Kerr, *Personality and Conflict in Jamaica*, revised edition, London and Kingston, 1963.
A. C. Kinsey *et al.*, *Sexual Behaviour in the Human Male*, N.Y., 1948.
B. Lasker, *Race Prejudice in Children*, N.Y., 1929.
Mathew Lewis, *Journal of a West India Prospector 1815–17*, London, 1929.
J. G. Leyburn, *The Haitian People*, Yale, 1941.
R. Linton, *The Study of Man*, N.Y., 1937.
K. L. Little, *Negroes in Britain*, London, 1947.
Henry Long, *History of Jamaica*, London, 1774.
I. D. MacCrone, *Race Attitudes in South Africa*, London, 1937.
A. Metraux, *Voodoo in Haiti*, London, 1959.
J. Mooney, 'The Ghost Dance Religion', *14th Annual Report 1892–3, Pt. 2, American Bureau of Ethnology*, Washington, 1896.

L. B. Namier, *England in the Age of the American Revolution*, London, 1930.

Katrin Norris, *Jamaica : The Search for Identity*, Oxford, 1962.

Lord Olivier, *Jamaica : The Blessed Island*, London, 1936.

— *The Myth of Governor Eyre*, London, 1933.

H. Paget, 'The Free Village System in Jamaica', *Jamaican Historical Review*, Vol. I, No. 1.

Orlando Patterson, *The Sociology of Slavery*, London, 1967.

Margery Perham, *The Colonial Reckoning*, London, 1963.

J. M. Phillips, *Jamaica : Its Past and Present State*, London, 1843.

Donald Pierson, *Negroes in Brazil*, Chicago, 1942.

A. C. Powell, '*Marching Blacks*', N.Y., 1945.

L. J. Ragatz, *The Decline of the Planter Class in the British Caribbean 1763–1834*, N.Y., 1928.

— *A Guide for the Study of British Caribbean History*, Washington, 1932.

R. Q. Rattray, *Akan-Ashanti Folk Tales*, Oxford, 1930.

Registrar-General's Report, Jamaica, 1942.

Report of Jamaican Nutrition Committee, Jamaica, 1937.

Report of the Middle Class Unemployment Committee, Jamaica, 1941.

Report of the Royal West India Commission, H.M.S.O., London, 1945.

G. W. Roberts, *The Population of Jamaica*, Cambridge, U.K., 1957.

C. S. Roundell, *England and Her Subject Races with special reference to Jamaica*, London, 1866.

Vera Rubin, ed., *Carribbean Studies : A Symposium*, Seattle, 1960.

—, ed., *Social and Cultural Pluralism in the Carribbean*, N.Y., 1960.

Michael Schofield, *Sociological Aspects of Homosexuality*, London, 1965.

B. Semmel, *The Governor Eyre Controversy*, London, 1962.

Sir Philip Sherlock, *The West Indies*, London, 1966.

—and J. H. Parry, *A Short History of the West Indies*, London, 1956.

T. S. Simey, *Welfare and Planning in the West Indies*, Oxford, 1946.

G. E. Simpson, 'Sexual and Familial Institutions in Northern Haiti', *American Anthropologist*, Vol. 44, No. 4.

Sir Hans Sloane, *A Voyage to the Islands . . . and Jamaica*, London, 1707–25.

M. G. Smith, *West Indian Family Structure*, Seattle, 1962.

— *The Plural Society in the British West Indies*, California, 1965.

M. G. Smith, R. Augier and R. Nettleford, *The Ras Tafari Movement in Kingston, Jamaica*, Department of Extra-Mural Studies, U.W.I., Jamaica, 1960.

T. Southey, *Chronological History of the West Indies*, London, 1827.

James West, 'Plainville, U.S.A.', in Abram Kardiner, *The Psychological Frontiers of Society*, N.Y., 1945.

Eric Williams, *Capitalism and Slavery*, Chapel Hill, 1944.

— *The Negro in the Caribbean*, Washington, 1942.

F. E. Williams, 'The Vailala Madness in Retrospect', in *Essays Presented to C. G. Seligman*, London, 1934.

INDEX